OCRACOKE

OCRACOKE

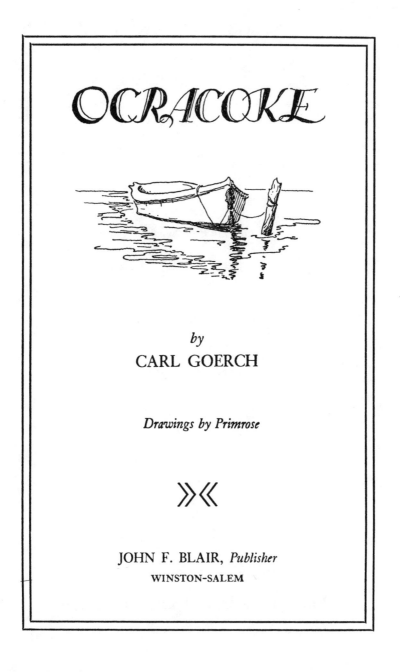

by

CARL GOERCH

Drawings by Primrose

〉〉《《

JOHN F. BLAIR, *Publisher*

WINSTON-SALEM

Eleventh Printing, 1989

ISBN 0-89587-031-2

Printed in the United States of America

To
The Rondthalers
(Alice and Theodore)

FOR MANY YEARS OUTSTANDING CITIZENS OF THE IS-
LAND, INTERESTED IN ALL WORTHWHILE PROJECTS.

Contents

CONTENTS

Ocracoke As He Knew It

The late Carl Goerch loved all of North Carolina. The General Assembly recognized this long love affair by naming him "Mr. North Carolina." He had visited all fifty states and fifty-two foreign countries, but if you asked him his favorite spot on earth, he no doubt would have said Ocracoke.

He first wrote this book in 1956, so some of the statements included herein are no longer accurate. For example, other means of transportation to the island and other services are available. But rather than destroy the charm he has captured here, we ask you to see Ocracoke through his eyes and learn how things used to be.

This is not a travelogue but a love story about our father and Ocracoke. Read it and enjoy both him and his impressions of the island in the 1950s.

DORIS GOERCH HORTON

SIBYL GOERCH POWE

BEAUFORT COUNTY

INLAND WATERWAY

MATTAMUSKEET LAKE

261

HYDE COUNTY

PAMLICO R.

PAMLICO SOUND

HATTERAS

PAMLICO COUNTY

NEUSE R.

1

CARTERET COUNTY

70

CORE SOUND

ATLANTIC OCEAN

4

3

CAPE LOOKOUT

✸ OCRACOKE
1 PORTSMOUTH
2 ATLANTIC
3 BEAUFORT
4 MOREHEAD

Location of the Island

The first thing you probably want to know about Ocracoke is its location and something about its topography.

Study for a moment the map of the eastern part of North Carolina which appears on the opposite page. Note the narrow strip of land that runs along the outer edge of the coast. This area is known as the outer banks and is separated from the mainland by several sounds, the largest of which are Albemarle and Pamlico.

And let me tell you something: when there's a strong northeaster blowing, these sounds really can get rough. I've been across Pamlico Sound in various types of vessels and it isn't at all unusual for them to slap bottom while in the trough of high waves. These waterways for the most part are rather shallow, and the average depth is around six feet.

The outer banks are pierced by a number of inlets through which boats of comparatively light draught can pass. Among these are Oregon, Hatteras, Ocracoke, Drum and Beaufort, some of which are shown on the map. There are others further down the coast. From

11

time to time a severe storm will come along and close up some of the smaller inlets and create new ones.

At some points, the expanse of water between the banks and the mainland is more than 20 miles wide; at others the distance is less than a mile.

Ocracoke is the island just below Hatteras. In order to do away with any possible confusion, let me explain that the name refers to both the island and the village. The island is sixteen miles long and ranges in width from half a mile to two miles. The greatest width is near the southern extremity where the village is located.

There is considerable vegetation on the sound side —scrub pines, water oaks, wax myrtles, yaupon, red cedar and, in many places, heavy growth of underbrush and marsh grass. There also are a number of fig trees, and the fruit from these is simply delicious. Fig preserves and hot biscuits—there's something that really is fittin'.

The vegetation does not extend all the way across the island to the beach on the ocean side. At some points the sand flats are a mile wide and these are completely bare of any growth whatsoever. Here and there a sand dune rears its head, but with the exception of these, the terrain is flat. When a strong wind is blowing, the sand can give you quite a beating.

Starting at Hatteras Inlet, which is at the northern end of the island, you come to a spot where a Coast Guard station was formerly located. Erosion brought the surf right up to the front door of the building and eventually undermined it. Finally, it collapsed.

Last time I was there, no signs of the station were visible.

And therein lies one of the peculiarities of our beaches along the North Carolina coast. They have a tendency to build up in some places and wear away in others. It all depends upon the winds and tides.

The population of the island is centered in the village of Ocracoke, located around Silver Lake, one of the

13

finest little harbors you'll find anywhere along the Atlantic coast. Its outlet is into the sound and is less than 200 feet in width. The lake itself is about a quarter-mile wide and is in the form of a circle. Dozens of boats, used for sport and commercial fishing, are tied to the docks or are moored to stakes a short distance from shore. During the height of the shrimping season, with bad weather prevailing outside, I've seen more than a hundred boats in the harbor.

The village proper is located around the lake. This includes stores, residences, Coast Guard station, lighthouse, power plant and ice factory. The population is about 525 and this figure hasn't changed much in recent years. During the summer months it is augmented by many vacationists. In the spring and fall, fishermen are there in large numbers, and this also is true of duck and goose hunters who arrive on the island in the wintertime.

Until World War II there was no pavement of any kind. You had to walk through sandy lanes and paths and, during dry weather, this sand could get uncomfortably deep, making walking a rather strenuous task. A naval installation was in operation at Ocracoke during the war and was responsible for the construction of about two miles of ten-foot-wide pavement from the naval buildings, near the Coast Guard station, to a munitions dump. This was followed several years later by more pavement around the lake. Altogether there now are about five miles of paved road in the village. Elsewhere the deep sand still prevails in the lanes which wind through the heavy growth of dwarfed trees.

In addition to the paving in the village, there now also is a road which runs practically the entire length of the island—from a short distance below Hatteras Inlet down to the village of Ocracoke. This piece of paving often suffers damage from severe storms, but the State Highway Department does a good job of maintenance and repairs are made quickly.

It's an interesting drive amid sand dunes and a wide expanse of bare sand which stretches out toward the ocean.

Prior to this stretch of paved road, automobiles were rather few and far between on the island. Now, however, there is considerable travel as people come from all parts of the country to see what Ocracoke looks like.

How to Get There

Approximately eighty miles northeast of Ocracoke is Elizabeth City, metropolis of the Albemarle section and a most attractive and progressive town. You can drive from there to Nags Head and Oregon Inlet. A wonderful new bridge was completed across the inlet in 1964. On the other side there's a paved road all the way to the village of Hatteras. On your right you'll see Bodie Island lighthouse. You'll pass through the Pea Island game refuge and, if you happen to be driving through that area during the proper season of the year, you'll see wild ducks, geese and swan by the tens of thousands. There are several picturesque little towns along your route—Rodanthe, Waves, Salvo, Avon, Buxton, Frisco and others. The pavement ends at Hatteras and from there you drive through the sand to a point near the inlet. A ferry now operates across Hatteras Inlet and will land you safely on Ocracoke Island. Then there's a thirteen-mile drive over a paved road to the village.

That's one way to get there.

Another popular route is to go by way of Atlantic.

This is an attractive town of about 800 population, approximately 30 miles northeast of Beaufort. On the way you'll pass through the villages of Otway, Smyrna, Davis, Stacy and Sea Level. At the last-named place is a modern, well-staffed and well-equipped hospital which was donated to the community by the Taylor brothers—Dan, William, Albert and Leslie. They were born and reared here and then went to Norfolk and West Palm Beach, where they've made a lot of money, and they have done many beneficial things for the folks in the old home town.

The Taylor brothers started a ferry service in the spring of 1960 between Atlantic and Ocracoke, making one round trip a day. Three years later, the State Highway Department took over the ferry and it now operates between Cedar Island and Ocracoke, making two round trips a day.

If you like to fly, you can charter a plane at Beaufort and it will take you up the banks to Ocracoke in about forty minutes. The huge sand flat, just east of the village, makes a dandy landing field. Hundreds of private planes land there every year.

And, of course, if you have your own boat, it's no trouble to get to the island although you may get stuck in the mud several times if you're not careful.

How It Got Its Name

If you make inquiry regarding the origin of the name, Ocracoke, the chances are that you will receive one of two answers.

The first is based on legend, pure and simple. The second, according to those individuals who have done some research work, is authentic.

Here's the legend:

Edward Teache ("Blackbeard") was a holy terror to shipping along the Atlantic coast during Colonial days. His maraudings became so extensive that the people appealed to Governor Spottswood of Virginia and begged him to do something about the situation. The Governor offered a reward of 100 pounds for the capture of the pirate. He also ordered Lieutenant Robert Maynard of the English Navy to take action.

In command of two ships, the Lieutenant sailed down the Carolina coast from Hampton Roads. He had obtained word that Teache was last seen somewhere near Ocracoke. And, sure enough, that's exactly where he was.

Somehow or other word had also got to Teache that

Maynard was heading his way. News to this effect arrived late in the afternoon, after dusk. Teache was scared to leave his anchorage near the island at night because of the treacherous shoals, but he hoped to make his escape just as soon as it was light enough for him to see his way out.

During the long night of waiting, Teache paced the deck of his ship, hoping that daylight would come before the arrival of the British ships. Several times he is said to have shouted, "Oh, crow, cock!" He knew that when he heard the first cock's crow his ship would soon be on its way.

When dawn came, however, it was too late. Lieutenant Maynard's ships were standing by. A battle took place and it is said that the Lieutenant and Teache engaged in man-to-man combat. Teache was defeated. The story goes that his head was cut off, fastened to the bowsprit of one of Maynard's vessels and taken up to Bath where there was quite a celebration. Some authorities state the ships went to Williamsburg and that the celebration took place there. It probably didn't make much difference to Teache; one place was just the same as the other to him.

It was from the words "Oh, crow, cock!" That Ocracoke is supposed to have received its name.

Nice little story, isn't it? Its only shortcoming is that despite the many times it has been told, it just isn't true.

Here is the generally accepted authentic version:

I've seen maps dating back to 1676 and 1680 which showed the island and designated it as Wocokon, Woccocock and, later, Ocacock. Some of these maps were made a hundred years before Teache was engaged in the practice of piracy.

The Woccos (and there are several ways of spelling this name) were a small tribe of Indians inhabiting this part of the outer banks, and it was for them that the island was named.

The Boat Trip Across the Sound

In the so-called "good old days" the big majority of visitors to Ocracoke made use of the mail boat in order to get to the island. This craft maintained a one-way-daily schedule, leaving Atlantic at about noon and arriving at Ocracoke at 3:30. On the return trip it left Ocracoke at seven in the morning and arrived at Atlantic at about 10:30. It was replaced by the ferry system in 1963.

Maybe you'd like to read a description of the trip by mail boat. Here's an account of it which I wrote up about fifteen years ago.

You leave your car at Atlantic. While waiting for departure time, I'd suggest you take a look around the village and visit the places where fish, shrimp, oysters, etc., are handled. Cecil Morris' store is in the center of town and is the largest merchandising establishment. Clayton Fulcher is one of the big operators in the fish business.

There's a nice little restaurant, and you can get a

good meal before boarding the boat. Or you can take some sandwiches along and eat them on the trip.

Inasmuch as the federal government asks for bids every year in connection with hauling the mail back and forth between Atlantic and Ocracoke, there isn't much use in describing the boat, because by the time you decide to visit the island, the description might be obsolete. The name of the craft that carried the mail last year was the *Dolphin*, captained by Ansley O'Neal. She's about forty-five feet in length. Ansley had a lot of engine trouble last year and had to hire substitute boats to carry the mail. These, for the most part, were shrimpers, about thirty-eight feet from stem to stern.

During the summer months the mail boat will carry as many as thirty-five passengers. At other times there may be only four or five aboard.

In addition to mail and passengers, the boat also hauls considerable freight. This is stowed away in the hold and on deck.

There are benches on which you can sit with a fair degree of comfort. If the boat is crowded, you can find a resting place on an empty fish box or take your seat on some of the packages of freight. If it starts raining, everybody tries to get down in the cabin. Those who are unsuccessful in doing this cheerfully remain on deck and get soaked.

There's usually an awning over the afterdeck. If you can't get under the awning you stand a fine chance of getting one of the best sunburns you've ever had.

Doesn't sound particularly appealing, does it? However, I don't believe I've ever heard of anybody complaining. Everybody seems to enjoy the trip.

When the mail, the passengers and the freight have been stowed aboard, the boat backs away from the dock and heads out into Core Sound. Over on the outer banks you can see the Coast Guard station. On your left, about half an hour after you leave Atlantic, is Cedar Island. Clayton Fulcher and some others are hoping that one of these days the State will operate a ferry between Ocracoke and Cedar Island.

You see several crab pots, marked by buoys. These are attended daily by the owners. Also quite a number of shrimp boats going around in circles. They're dredging for clams. The boat comes to Wainwright Channel. On your left again is a big two-story building situated on the tiniest kind of an island. This is Harbor Island. The structure was erected some twenty years ago as a fishing and hunting club. With the passing of the years, it has been deserted and is slowly disintegrating. The roof is partly off, there are no window panes and no doors. Within the next few years the whole structure will probably fall to pieces. Not only the building but also the island will disappear. Irving Forbes and Lawrence Ballard, who were running the mail boat the last time I made the trip a few months ago, said they could remember when the island consisted of fifteen or twenty acres. Now there's less than an acre of it left. The rest has been submerged.

Shell Island, flat and deserted and a resting place for seagulls and other wild fowl, is a short distance from Harbor Island.

The distance from Atlantic to Ocracoke is slightly less than thirty miles, air line. The water route, however, is considerably farther than that, due to the twisting channels.

The boat approaches Portsmouth, the island just

27

below Ocracoke. Half a mile out from shore stands a Negro man in a skiff. The Post Office Department hires him to meet the boat every trip and take the mail ashore. The water is so shallow that the mail boat itself cannot get any closer to the little pier at Portsmouth.

The Negro's name is Henry Picott and he receives a salary of $50 a month for this little job.

There are only seventeen people living on Portsmouth Island. Most of them are old and rather feeble. As a matter of fact, Henry, age 59, is the youngest man there.

Miss Dorothy Mae Salter is temporary postmaster, having succeeded her mother who retired a few months ago. The total cost to the Government for bringing the mail to these seventeen residents of Portsmouth is $1,900 a year. Sounds high, but it can't be done any cheaper, and the residents of Portsmouth are just as much entitled to daily mail delivery as you are.

Miss Salter was aboard when I made the trip. She got into Henry's skiff, along with her suitcase, two crates containing milk, another containing some bread and several other smaller packages. Then Henry pushed his skiff away from our craft and started poling back to shore.

Portsmouth is probably the most isolated place along the entire Atlantic coast. Inlets to the north and south prevent any kind of motor vehicle traffic. No motorboats can land because of the shallow water; only a light skiff can make it. Once or twice there's been a channel dug to the pier but this doesn't do much

28

good because the first storm that comes along proceeds to fill it up.

There are no stores on the island and the only thing you can buy is a postage stamp. Every once in a while somebody gets into a skiff and rows to Ocracoke (five miles) for canned goods and other commodities. There's no school because there are no children. There's a church but most of the residents are ailing, so services are held in the homes once a month by a preacher who visits the island from the town of Sea Level.

The boat crosses Ocracoke Inlet and proceeds up the sound side of Ocracoke Island, about a half-mile from shore. Three or four sand dunes on our right. Then the village, with the lighthouse and Coast Guard station dominating the scene. The entrance into the harbor of Silver Lake is only about 200 feet wide, and the dock in front of the post office, where the mail boat always lands, is just a short distance beyond.

You've arrived at Ocracoke.

That's an account of the trip as you would have made it twenty or more years ago. At the present time there are only seven people still living on the island of Portsmouth. A boat arrives from Ocracoke once a week with provisions, other supplies, and mail. A preacher from the mainland holds services once a month.

Your Reception on the Island

Yes, that's the way most folks used to make the trip to the island before it was possible to drive from Nags Head to Ocracoke by way of ferries and paved roads.

The arrival of the mail boat was the big event of the day, just as the arrival of the ferry is today. Let's take another look into the past and see if I can bring you a picture of the scene that used to take place at Ocracoke when the mail boat put in its appearance. The same scene is re-enacted today when the ferry arrives.

Here's a continuation of the article which described the trip across the sound.

The mail boat is due at about 3:30. Shortly after three o'clock people begin to gather at the dock in front of the post office or in the stores just a short distance away. Jake is there with his taxicab, ready to take the visitors and their luggage to the hotel or wherever they want to go. The postmaster, Mrs. Elizabeth

Howard, is on the job, ready to sort out the mail immediately upon its arrival. (Note: the Government says there is no such word as "postmistress." Mrs. Howard is postmaster.) Stanley Wahab, an Ocracoker who made good up in Baltimore and returned to the island to spend the rest of his days, is among those present. Ike and Walt O'Neal, Jones Williams, Hunter Robinson, Captain Tom Howard, Charlie McWilliams and many others are there, including a dozen or more young folks playing around.

They exchange the news of the day because it's just about the only opportunity they have for swapping conversation on an extensive scale.

Usually it's some small boy, perched precariously on a piling at the end of the pier, who is first to glimpse the boat swinging around the point and getting ready to come in through the narrow entrance of the harbor.

"Here she comes!" he calls out.

People leave the stores. They rise from the boxes or crates on which they have been sitting and begin walking out on the pier. The boat by this time is halfway across Silver Lake and is turning in toward her landing place.

The first thing that observers on the shore are interested in is sizing up the number of people aboard. Passengers are equally interested in sizing up the natives.

The boat swings slowly up alongside the dock and is made fast. Suitcases and other baggage are thrown out. Passengers clamber over the low railing and onto the pier. Some of them are Ocracokers, returning home. Perhaps also a commercial traveling man or two. Visitors who have been on the island before and have become acquainted with some of the residents, exchange hearty greetings.

There's a general stirring around as baggage is claimed and the mail is taken to the post office. Suitcases are loaded into waiting vehicles. Gradually the crowd moves over to the post office. The mail is put up in short order. Trucks and jeeps move off. People begin to walk away. Soon the crowd has dispersed entirely and the big event of the day is over.

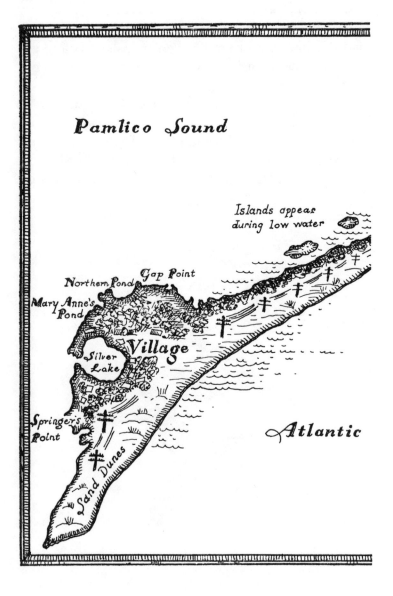

Pamlico Sound

Islands appear
during low water

Gap Point

Northern Pond

Mary Anne's
Pond

Village

Silver
Lake

Atlantic

Springer's
Point

Sand Dunes

Hatteras ↗
New Inlet, cut in 1956

Abandoned
Coast Guard
Station

Sand Dunes

N

W   E

S

Ocean

The Island of Ocracoke

First Impressions

Ocracokers eat supper early. Visitors at hotels and boarding houses have to do the same thing if they want to be fed. There's none of this foolishness of keeping dining rooms open until nine o'clock in the evening. You eat at six, if you want a hot supper, or else you don't eat at all.

No, I'll take that back. Sometimes fishermen remain out on the beach until after the regular supper hour. They may not return to their hotel 'til nine or ten o'clock but they still can get something to eat.

It was left on the table for them. Left there at six o'clock. Naturally everything is stone cold (although you can get a cup of hot coffee) but food tastes good at Ocracoke regardless of whether it is hot or cold—especially after you've been standing out in the salt air for several hours and are thoroughly weary.

We'll take it for granted that you arrived on the island on the mail boat. By the time you get to your hotel or boarding house it's five o'clock. You unpack and clean up a bit. Promptly at six the supper bell rings. It may have been on your program to take a drink or two, relaxing after the boat trip, and then sitting down to your evening meal at about eight o'clock. There's no objection to your taking a drink, if you do it privately, nor is there any objection to your relaxing, but you'll have to attend to this before six o'clock.

And another thing; you don't have to study over a lengthy menu when you get into the dining room. You'll find the food has already been placed on the table. The waitress comes up to you and asks: "What'll you have to drink?"

That's the only choice you have.

If you're on the island in the summertime, it's still light outside after supper, so you decide to take a walk and see what the place looks like.

You follow the ten-foot paved road and head for Silver Lake, a couple of hundred yards distant around a bend in the highway. Stumpy trees grow on either side of the road. Some of these are yaupons. A form of tea is made from the leaves and this is still relished occasionally by some people living on the outer banks. Visitors also.

The houses are entirely of frame structure, nicely painted and, for the most part, neat in appearance. Oleander trees grow in many of the yards. So do zinnias, hydrangeas and other blooms. Most of the yards are fenced in and the fences are in good repair.

When someone decides to build a new house nowadays he has to order the necessary lumber from Washington, New Bern, Beaufort or some other point on the mainland. Long ago, however, many homes on the

island were built of lumber salvaged from wrecked ships.

Occasionally, as you walk along, you meet a car or truck, or else a vehicle approaches from behind. This means you have to step off the pavement and stand in the sand on either side in order to let the jeep or truck pass. The occupants give either a slight wave of the hand or a cordial nod.

You observe this same friendliness on the part of everyone you meet along the road, young and old alike. All of them have a brief word of greeting, and none seems especially curious about who you are or what your business might be. If you want to stop someone and engage in a conversation about things pertaining to the island, he'll stay with you as long as you want him to.

Their attire is along simple lines. In the summertime most of the men wear a T-shirt and pair of duck trousers. Shoes are generally worn, although when mariners are working on a boat or along the docks or maybe around the house, the shoes very often are discarded. And I for one don't blame them for doing so because, to my way of thinking, shoes are superfluous on the island as an item of wearing apparel.

It just naturally feels good to walk through the sand, barefooted, and many visitors take off their shoes on arrival on the island and never put them on again until they are ready to leave.

The women wear plain dresses. Twenty-five years or so ago they, too, frequently went barefooted while going from one place to another, but you don't see that any more. Sunbonnets may still be seen, and wide-brimmed hats are popular because they help keep off the rays of the sun.

Sundays, when folks go to church, you'll find everyone dressed up just as they are in your own town.

People on the island dress with one principal thought in mind—comfort. They don't go in for anything fancy in the way of apparel. I've never seen an Ocracoke woman of mature years dressed in slacks or shorts, and I've never seen an Ocracoke man wearing Bermuda shorts or other type of summer attire so much in vogue at more sophisticated resorts.

As you start walking around Silver Lake you come to what might best be described as the down-town business section of Ocracoke. Here are the post office, the ice and electric plant, three stores, storage tanks for gasoline and diesel fuel, most of the docks and, just a short distance away, the Coast Guard station. All on the north side of the lake.

If you're hungering for conversation you usually can find several small groups of men sitting in front of the stores or on the docks.

It's a rather busy scene. Customers are entering and leaving the stores. Men are at work on boats tied up along shore. The engines in the power and ice plant offer a background of noise of which one soon loses consciousness.

Altogether there are four small stores on the island and their stocks of merchandise consist principally of things to eat. Also a sizable quantity of marine supplies. One can buy a limited number of articles of wearing

apparel. Also soft drinks, tobacco and cigarettes, toilet accessories and so on, but that's about all. Most of the population manage to get to the mainland at least once a year and these expeditions are in the nature of intensive shopping trips. Washington, Beaufort and Morehead City are favored with most of this patronage.

Time and again, as you walk along, you can't help but be impressed with the attention property owners give to the cultivation of flowers. Near the southern end of the village you'll see several yards with a most beautiful profusion of blossoms of a wide variety.

Practically everyone has at least a few flowers growing in the front or at the sides of their homes.

The lighthouse property, with its well-kept grounds and buildings, is one of the principal points of interest on the island. It is the oldest in service along the Atlantic coast.

Farther along you'll see vestiges of Pamlico Inn, for many years the most popular hostelry on the island. Operated by Captain Bill Gaskill and his family, it was known far and wide for its fine seafood. Captain Bill died over forty years ago. Storms blew down the hotel. The water tank and a few pilings out in the water are just about all that's left.

At the extreme southerly end of the village is what is known as Springer's Point. It was here that the pirate, Edward Teache, is supposed to have had a hide-out, and it was close by that he was killed by Lieutenant Maynard. It is also here that Blackbeard is supposed to have buried some of his treasure.

There's been a lot of digging throughout the years in this locality, but thus far no money has been found. As a matter of fact, those folks, who have done some research work in connection with the history of Ocracoke, are doubtful that Teache ever had a place of residence at Springer's Point.

Another outstanding spot of interest is the Coast Guard station, a large frame structure, painted white, in close proximity to the little channel which serves as an outlet for Silver Lake into the sound. Usually you'll find one or more Coast Guard boats tied to the piers in front of the station. It is located across the lake from the light house.

Children on bicycles . . . ponies wandering around loose and grazing in front yards . . . sea gulls floating aloft in the southwesterly breeze . . . the chug-chug of motors in boats . . . quacking of ducks and geese as they cross your path . . . all combine to create an atmosphere that is different from anything you'll find elsewhere along our coast.

By the time you have finished your walk you'll have a pretty good idea of what Ocracoke is like and your first impression in most instances will be favorable. That is, if you like simple living without any of the fancy frills that you will find at the average summer resort.

Pamlico Sound

U.S.
Park
Service

Engine + Repair Shop

U.S. Coast
Guard
Station

Stores, Fish-Houses

Ice + Power Plant

Community
Store

Post Office

Silver
Lake

Fish-House

Nurse

Lighthouse

Styrons

Silver Lake
Inn

Sound Front
Inn

Church

The Village
of
Ocracoke

Grave of Ann Howard
Graves of British Sailors

N
W E
S

old Navy Amunition Dump

School & Recreation Hall

Church

Jake's Place

Wahab Hotel

Atlantic Ocean
one half mile →

You Like It or You Don't

I know people—plenty of them—who visit Ocracoke at least once a year. They've been doing this for fifteen, twenty or thirty years and they'll probably keep it up as long as they're able to travel.

To their way of thinking, it's one of the grandest places in the world. They love everything about it, including the deep sand and the mosquitoes, and they wouldn't swap it for Miami, Newport or the Riviera.

On the other hand, I've known people to arrive on the mail boat at 4:30 p.m., and they could hardly wait until the seven o'clock boat left the following morning. One look at the place was enough for them and they wanted no part of it.

It all depends upon the type of person who visits the island.

If you are the restless type, if you've got to be constantly on the go, if you like gay night clubs or gambling joints, if you have to be near a golf course in order to be happy, if you enjoy classy restaurants serving

exotic viands to the accompaniment of a muted orchestra—if these are the kind of things that give you
pleasure, then I urge you by all means to stay away
from Ocracoke, because you won't like it.

On the other hand—

If you can be content doing absolutely nothing in
the way of recreation or amusement, if you like to
get up early in the morning and enjoy the restful
atmosphere which is such an important part of life
on Ocracoke, if you enjoy strolling aimlessly around,
watching the leisurely activity around Silver Lake, if

4   49

you like to dress simply and go barefooted without attracting any particular attention, if you appreciate good seafood, going bathing or fishing when the mood to do so makes it desirable, if you want to get just as far away as possible from all the hullabaloo, tenseness and excitement of modern living—if these things appeal to you then you'll enjoy Ocracoke to the fullest extent.

What is there to do besides the things I've just mentioned?

What more do you want?

You'll find comfortable accommodations, excellent food, fine fishing and hunting, friendly people, bathing in either the ocean or sound, and dancing practically every night in the village dance hall.

Used to be that square dances were held every Saturday night in the school recreation room, but the young folks today seem to prefer jitterbugging, doing the twist, and other modern dances to the old-timey type.

If these things don't sound interesting, stay away from Ocracoke because you'll be miserable and bored to death during your stay on the island.

If they do appeal to you, you'll have a fine time every minute you're there. And when you leave the place you'll feel more rested and relaxed than you have felt in a long time. Not only that, but you'll probably also gain seven or eight pounds before your departure.

Land of Romance

Are you a member of the feminine sex?

Have you been unable to interest any male in making a proposal of marriage?

Would you like to get married in a hurry?

If so—go to Ocracoke.

Here's why:

When you go to Carolina Beach, Wrightsville, Atlantic Beach, Nags Head or some other resort that attracts thousands of visitors every season, you run into competition. There may be prettier and more attractive girls around than you. Not only that, but there are so many diversified things to do—playing tennis or golf, riding horseback, spending a lot of time in night clubs, or at beach parties, gala balls, and so on. All that's a lot of fun but it's not too easy to bring real romance into such a picture.

But at Ocracoke it's different, and many people—many women, especially—have found it out.

In looking over the registers in some of the motels and hotels I've been impressed with the number of ladies who have gone to the island without male

51

escorts. In groups of two, three, four or half a dozen. Occasionally a solitary figure. Many of them have gone there with a definite purpose in mind—to catch a man. And undoubtedly many have been successful in doing this.

You, too, can be successful. It may not work on the first trip down to the island, or the second trip, or the third trip, but it will work ultimately.

I'm willing to guarantee it.

Let's see if we can give you a good description of what takes place.

Several men have gone there to spend their vacation and do a little fishing. They've been out all day. They return to the hotel, somewhat weary. Perhaps they take a couple of drinks before eating supper. Then comes a big meal, following which they sit out on the porch or on the cement wall in front of the hotel. They're satisfied, contented, at peace with the world. A gentle breeze is blowing. There is an aura of light far off in the distance. It develops into a full moon, slowly and impressively rising out of the ocean, and it is heralded by silver ripples extending toward the shore.

Under these circumstances, thoughts of romance are bound to pervade a man's mind. If they don't, he just isn't human.

So what follows?

One of the men—maybe all of them for that matter— glances about him. Over in one corner of the porch he sees you sitting, demure and silent. It may be true that you are slightly cross-eyed, that you have a figure like a barn door and that you stammer when you talk, but that doesn't make any difference.

You're a woman.

You're the only unattached woman within range. He strolls over and says: "Good evening, my name is So-and-so." You tell him your name. He asks where you're from, and you tell him. After a few more remarks of this nature he says, "It's such a beautiful night, wouldn't you like to take a little walk out toward the beach?"

Certainly you would.

You start off together, and from then on, sister, it's up to you. The whole deal is in your hands.

This same thing has happened time and again on Ocracoke Island. It has resulted in numerous marriages and has brought people together who otherwise might never have spoken to each other.

If you've got romance on your mind, here's the place where it really will bear fruit. If you can't make the grade at Ocracoke, you might just as well give up and resign yourself to being an old maid.

Ocracoke As I First Knew It

The first time I visited Ocracoke was during the summer of 1915.

In those days there were sailing vessels (sharpies) with auxiliary motors that operated on a regular schedule between Washington and the island. One boat left Washington Wednesday evening at eight o'clock, the other left Saturday evening, same time.

It was an all-night trip. Nobody thought seriously of going to sleep, although some folks spread blankets on the deck and managed to get in several naps of short duration.

You couldn't do much sleeping, however, with a constant jabbering of conversation going on throughout the night. Then, too, there were no rules or regulations against taking a drink, and this helped enliven things considerably.

As a general thing, it was a bedraggled looking bunch of passengers when they finally arrived at Captain Bill Gaskill's wharf at 6:30 in the morning.

Captain Bill would be on hand to help dock the boat and see that baggage was taken care of.

His hotel was known as Pamlico Inn. In those days there was no inside plumbing. This also was true of the Bragg house and other boarding houses. Rough boards comprised walls and ceilings of the guest rooms. Furniture was of the simplest kind. There was no electricity.

Doesn't sound very appealing, does it? But in those days folks knew what to expect and nobody ever thought of complaining.

Silver Lake wasn't in existence. The village was divided by a creek and, as I recall, there was some slight social distinction depending on which side of the creek the residents lived.

People didn't come to Ocracoke from all parts of the country, the way they do now; they came mostly from points in eastern North Carolina—Washington, Greenville, Wilson, Williamston, etc. Only an occasional fisherman or hunter would come from greater distances.

Pamlico Inn was on the sound side of the island. A long pier—100 feet or more, as I recall—stretched out over shallow water to the channel where it was possible for the boats to tie up and load and unload.

Then as now, Ocracoke was famous for its seafood, and the meals that Miss Annie (Captain Bill's wife) prepared for the guests were out of this world.

Every afternoon, 'long about two o'clock, Bill would call out that the truck was ready. The truck had no sides or top to it. It was used as a conveyance to take bathers over to the beach, more than a mile away. There it remained for a couple of hours, and then the bathers would be hauled back to the inn again. It was a rough journey. A good friend of mine, Claude Gardner of Washington, was sitting on the rear end of the truck on one trip. He bounced into the air when the truck hit a hole, broke his back as he struck the edge of the truck coming down, and died before he could be taken to the hospital in Washington.

When you were at Ocracoke in those days, you really were ex communicado. The Coast Guard had a telephone line up and down the banks but most of the time it was out of order.

The mail boat, capable of carrying about twenty passengers, operated between Atlantic and Ocracoke, maintaining a regular schedule. There was also spasmodic freight service from Engelhard.

Captain Bill had a pavilion near the pier and this was the scene of square dances 'most every night during the summer months. Ocracokers and visitors alike joined in the fun.

Those were the days of Big Ike O'Neal, Big Ben Garrish, Simey O'Neal and other wonderful characters. You may think that there are funny comedians in the theatrical world today, but to our way of thinking, none of them could compare with Simey. His imitation of a goat would drive people into hysterics.

No radio, no television, no airplanes, no paving of any kind. Horses and cows roaming wild in much larger numbers than is the case now.

And let me tell you something else. That trip across

the sound could be just about as rough a voyage as you can imagine. Under a full head of sail, with the deck careening at a crazy angle, with the fore part of the vessel slapping down into the trough of the sea to the accompaniment of a shower of heavy spray over the deck—it really was something.

Nowadays people go down to Ocracoke for the week end, but in the era which I am trying to describe, they never went for less than a whole week. That was the minimum. In the big majority of instances they stayed at least two weeks, and sometimes people remained during the entire summer.

Things You Won't Find on Ocracoke

It has been said many times that the people who live on Ocracoke Island are as happy and contented as you can find anywhere.

One evening, during a recent visit to the island, several of us amused ourselves by making a list of things which you won't find on Ocracoke.

Here are some of them:

Policeman	Florist
Traffic light	Billboard
Elevator	Sidewalk
Pool hall	Bakery
Brick building	Bank
Chain store	Beer parlor
Hospital	Jail
Parking meters	Book store
Golf course	Bowling alley
Lawyer	Dancing school
Doctor	Dentist
Furniture store	Diaper service
Drug store	Funeral home
Printer	Hardware store

Life on the Island

Life on Ocracoke moves along at a leisurely pace and is less complicated than it is on the mainland. There isn't that tenseness, excitement, hurry and bustle that you find in your big cities or even in smaller towns.

People work long hours but they take their time in doing things. Stores on the island don't close on Wednesday afternoons nor do they take off the entire day on Saturdays. Neither do they open their doors at 9 a.m. and close them at 5:30 p.m.

No, sir. They open shortly after daybreak and remain open until nine and ten o'clock at night. One reason for the late hour of closing is that the stores are meeting places for the islanders. They sit on the porches or steps and remain there until they get sleepy and feel an urge to go home and to bed.

What do they talk about? Mostly about local events; fishing, hunting, somebody building a new boat, and so on. If there's some particular event of national or international interest they'll talk about that, too, but for the most part the conversation has to do with Ocracoke and Ocracokers.

Practically every woman, if she is physically able, does her own housework. She, too, is an early riser and gets up around 5:30 in the morning.

Many homes have radios, and there are several that have television sets. The principal recreation is listening to these, visiting close-by neighbors and sitting in porch swings. From time to time there are church socials or entertainments at the schoolhouse and these always are well attended.

No regular beauty parlors are to be found on the island but there's a beautician who can give permanents and other cosmetic treatments. Not only that but

there are several other women who can do this kind of work and don't mind helping out friends and neighbors.

Prices are about half of what you pay on the mainland.

There's a barbershop which is operated by George Guthrie Jackson and is located near the Wahab Village Hotel. It's in a small building of its own, right next to George Guthrie's home. If you want a haircut you stand in front of the house and holler for George Guthrie to come out. If he's home and feels like working, he'll cut your hair for you. Most of the time, though, he isn't at home, but on Saturdays he spends the greater part of the day at his shop.

However, if you can't get service in the barbershop, there's usually a neighbor who can help you out. And there are quite a number of women who can give their husbands, brothers and sons just as good haircuts as they can get by a professional.

Ocracoke weather plays havoc with automobiles and trucks. This is due to the salt air and the blowing sand. Also to the strain of traveling over rough ground and deep sand. Sometimes, when the wide sand flat east of the village is flooded, the cars and trucks have to drive through water a foot deep in order to get over on the beach.

There's no regular garage on the island, but most of the men are mechanically minded and if anything goes wrong with your car, they can help you out.

Practically all the men know how to do carpentry work and they do their own repair work on house, barn or store. They can build a house from the ground up and turn out a right nice job. A few specialize in plumbing, electrical wiring and other jobs of that nature. Truck owners use their vehicles for hauling sand and other materials.

There's an important difference between workmen on the mainland and workmen on the island. So far as most people in your towns are concerned, they know exactly what they are going to do tomorrow, next week and even next year. They'll either be in a store or an office, they'll be working in some mill or factory, or they'll have some other kind of steady job.

Not so on Ocracoke, however. Ten or twelve people work in the stores, three work in the power plant, twenty-four are in the Coast Guard service, and a few devote all or most of their time to commercial fishing. However, the big payroll comes from the National Park Service. And then, too, there are about forty who receive pensions from the Coast Guard.

Most of the others do odd jobs of various kinds and their activities vary from day to day.

The people are closely knit. Intermarriage has made many of them related to one another. There's a fine spirit of co-operation and helpfulness. If anyone gets sick, neighbors help nurse him back to health. If anyone gets into some trouble or difficulty, he always can depend on getting help.

Here's how this works:

Several years ago, Calvin O'Neal's house burned down. He had been boiling tar preparatory to repairing the roof. The house caught fire and was completely

demolished. Almost before the embers had ceased smoking, neighbors and friends subscribed $800 to help Calvin get started in building a new home.

A woman becomes ill. She's in need of help and it is forthcoming promptly. A neighbor will help nurse her while another one will do the housework. No one ever thinks of accepting money for rendering this kind of service.

A man suddenly becomes sick. He must be moved to the hospital at Sea Level, Morehead City or perhaps Norfolk. It so happens that he is in somewhat of a financial pinch and is short of cash, but that doesn't make very much difference; neighbors contribute the necessary funds.

Last time I was at Ocracoke somebody was telling me about the death of a well known woman. (I've forgotten her name.) She had always been ready and willing to lend her services whenever and wherever they were needed to alleviate suffering and distress. She died on a Saturday morning. The community square dance Saturday night was called off immediately. It wasn't even necessary to pass the word around because everyone knew the dance wouldn't be held.

When a funeral occurs, all the stores on the island close.

Theirs is a peaceful, calm, placid life for the most part. About the only disturbing factor is an occasional storm, but the natives are used to this and it doesn't bother them particularly. They take storms in their stride.

During all the years I've been going to Ocracoke

there was only one telephone there and it was located in the Coast Guard station. The only time anyone ever tried to talk to a visitor on the island was when some kind of emergency demanded it. In 1960, however, the picture changed. The Carolina Telephone & Telegraph Company put in a phone line. Three telephones were in the original installation; now there are many more.

When you wake up in the morning in your home, you probably go downstairs, out on the front porch and pick up the morning paper which was delivered about daybreak. Ocracokers have to wait until after lunch time for their morning papers and these are early editions. No evening papers are received on the day of publication.

Folks keep up with the news by listening to the radio. As you walk through the village you hear radio programs emanating from almost every house you pass.

During the summer months the place is much livelier than at other times of the year. In addition to the visitors who stay at the hotels and boarding houses there are a number of mainlanders who have their own cottages. Then, too, scarcely a day passes that one or more yachts don't stop at the island—sometimes just to get some fuel, on other occasions to remain for several days.

With the exception of a few hunters and an occasional commercial traveling man there aren't many visitors during the winter. Ocracokers have the island more or less to themselves.

Their Form of Speech

Your average Ocracoker is fed up with people who make joking comments about the way he talks.

So would you be if you had been hearing outsiders try to mimic you throughout the years, particularly when they laugh as though they thought that they were doing something funny or clever.

Enough of anything can be too much.

However, in order to give you a comprehensive picture of the island and its people it is necessary to devote a little space to some peculiarities of speech found among the folks who live here and elsewhere on the outer banks.

Every section of the country has its peculiarities of speech. The people in New England talk differently from the way people in Michigan talk. Residents of Mississippi have an entirely different accent from the people who live in Ohio. You probably recall that there used to be a radio program in which the moderator could tell you where a person was from simply by having him say a few sentences.

The outstanding difference between speech at Ocracoke and points farther up state lies in the pronunciation of the letter "I." It is changed by the natives to "OI."

"Looks loike we'll be havin' good fishin' at hoigh toide this afternoon."

"What toime did you say it was?"

"Oi foinally landed the fish but he sure did foight."

After you've been on the "oisland" a while you get accustomed to this kind of talk and pay no more attention to it. Stay a few months and you'll be speaking the same way the natives do.

There are a number of expressions in use which sounded strange to me when I first started visiting Ocracoke. Here are a few of them:

"You fleech me." (Meaning flatter.)

"I disremember you ever tellin' me that."

"I don't fault you for saying that to him."

"First I hurt in the region of my stomach, but now the pain has swayzed around to the back."

"Don't yell at me: I heerd you."

"Shucks, that fish ain't fittin' to eat."

"He wanted to build hisself a new boat but Oi disencouraged him."

"The whole business has got me so mommicked that I don't know what to do." (Meaning puzzled or worried. It also is used like this: "He tried to do the job but mommicked things up generally.")

"The cow is in the powsture."

"You'll find Jim out in the yard somewhere near the chicken pound."

"Kind of ca'm (rhymes with ham) today but maybe the wind will come up in an hour or so."

"That's good some."

"What are you doin' of?"

"Ocean is mighty slick today."

The letter "W" is occasionally used instead of "V". Like this: "He lives up in Wirginia and has a wery good job."

Most of these expressions probably are new and strange to you. However, there are others in use on the mainland that are equally strange. Every section of North Carolina has its colloquialisms and, as I've just said, the same thing is true of every other state.

I'm not an expert at speech but I find that I can come pretty close to talking like an Ocracoker if I try to speak from the back of the throat instead of from near the front.

Try it and you'll see what I mean.

69

The Cost of Living

I have asked this question of a number of leading citizens in the village of Ocracoke—Ike O'Neal, Charlie McWilliams, Stanley Wahab, C. F. Boyette and others.

"Suppose a man down here has his home paid for. He is married and has two small children—say seven and nine years old. He also has a small garden and some chickens. How much cash money does it require for him to live comfortably?"

Most of the individuals of whom I asked this question said that not more than a hundred dollars a month would be required.

"If he had that amount of cash money coming in every thirty days," said Ike, "he'd have nothing to worry about. He'd get along very nicely and he and his family would be comfortable."

A little while later I happened to be at the Coast Guard station and mentioned this same subject to some of the boys there. Among them was Ben O'Neal, son of the late Simey O'Neal who was one of the most popular men on the island.

Ben snorted when I told him about the one hundred dollars a month.

"I should say a man could live comfortably on that," he said. "There's no reason why he shouldn't. But do you know that there are a number of men on this island who don't make anywhere near that amount?"

I told him I didn't.

"Well, it's the truth. There are some who never see more than forty or fifty dollars a month, especially when the fishing season is bad. But somehow or other they manage to get along."

"But how do they live on that small amount of money?" I asked him.

"I don't know," he replied frankly. "It's a mystery to me."

I told several other men what Ben had said and they agreed with him. I also asked them if they knew how a family could possibly live on such a small income. In every instance I got the same answer: "I don't know. It's something I've never been able to figure out."

Of course it is readily understandable that the cost of living on the island is much less than it is in cities and towns on the mainland. Come to think of it, though, that statement is not true in every instance. You have to pay more for soft drinks, ice cream, canned goods, fresh vegetables, meats, etc., on Ocracoke than you do in most places elsewhere, due to the cost of transportation. But in other respects it is cheaper. The average man and woman on Ocracoke spend comparatively little for wearing apparel. The only place that money can be spent for diversion or enter-

tainment is at the dance hall or at occasional social functions held in connection with some civic or church project.

The typical Ocracoke family raise their own vegetables. They have chickens. As a general rule they can catch all the fish they can eat. This also applies to oysters, clams, crabs and other seafood. If the man of the household doesn't hunt ducks or geese during the winter months the probabilities are that some kind neighbor will let the family have several fowl during the course of the hunting season.

Walk down the streets of most towns and you'll find all sorts of ways for spending money. Every place you pass is inviting you to come in and leave some of your cash. Then, too, there are many special events, such as big-time football, basketball and baseball games, supper and dance at a night club, week-end trips to some resort, and so on.

You don't meet up with these things on the island.

Another thing; when a man runs out of cash he always can get credit at one of the four stores in the village. When a customer's account gets too far in arrears and the store at which he has been trading threatens to cut him off, he can take his business elsewhere. This doesn't happen very often. As a general rule, things begin to pick up after a while and he is able to pay his debts.

An Ocracoker can't very well afford to dodge his financial obligations because he knows everyone on the island and everyone knows him. He can't permit himself to be labelled as a deadbeat. It is because of this fact that the little stores will extend him credit for a much longer period of time than would an establishment on the mainland.

In Raleigh, Wilson, Greensboro or Charlotte the probabilities are that your next-door neighbor doesn't know anything about your credit rating. On Ocracoke, everyone knows.

Along this same line, I was talking to a commercial traveler while on the island last spring. I asked him about the credit rating of merchants along the outer banks, practically all of whom do a rather small business.

"We never hesitate to sell them anything," was his reply. "They're mighty good pay. Sometimes, when the fishing is poor, they may get behind a bit but they'll always pay up in the end."

An Outsider's Point of View

Last summer, on one of my frequent visits to Ocracoke, I ran into John G. Perry, a lawyer from some town in up-state New York. Rochester, I believe it was, but I'm not exactly certain.

Anyway, Mr. Perry has been coming down to Ocracoke for a number of years. One evening, after supper, I asked him how it happened that he had picked Ocracoke as the place for his vacation. Here's what he had to say, and I'll try to quote his own words:

"I heard about Ocracoke from a friend in Rochester whose people came from North Carolina. He had been down here two or three times, hunting and fishing. From his description of the place, I decided I'd like to see what it was like, so I came down during the summer of 1947 and, with two or three exceptions, I've been coming here every summer since then. Hope I'll be able to continue doing so for a long time to come.

"I've been to various vacation resorts—all the way from Bar Harbor, Maine, to Miami, Florida, but I've

75

never found a spot where I can get such complete rest and relaxation as I can here. The trouble with most places is that there's too much going on. The big hotels have hostesses who try to drag you into bridge games, tennis matches, sight-seeing expeditions, horse-back riding and a lot of other things. There's a constant stream of people milling around you. All of them are heading for some sort of diversion. The general idea about that kind of vacation is to keep doing something. As a result of this, when you get back to your office, you feel in greater need of rest than you did before you left home.

"Now down here it's altogether different. Nobody bothers you, and you can do exactly as you please. If you want to spend most of the day sleeping, you're at liberty to do so. If you want to walk around, go fishing, take a dip in the ocean, spend your time reading, nobody will interfere with you. There isn't somebody around always nagging at you to do this, that or the other thing. As a matter of fact, nobody cares what you do.

"When I get away from here, I've had a complete rest. And, after all is said and done, that's what a vacation is supposed to do for you. I can get all the night-club entertainment, bridge-playing, theatre attractions and all other types of amusement and entertainment back home. Why should I wear myself out going to big resorts and engaging in that sort of thing?

"No, sir; not me. Ocracoke appeals to me and I'm better satisfied here than at any place I've ever been, so far as spending a vacation is concerned."

Everybody Is Equal

If former President Eisenhower were to disembark from the ferry and step out on the pier near the Coast Guard station, the first man to recognize him probably would say cordially: "Hello, Oike; glad to see you here."

Your average Ocracoker considers himself just as good as anybody else and rightfully so. People on the mainland may bow and scrape to other folks who are important politically, socially or otherwise but you won't find any of that kind of spirit in evidence on the island.

Lindsay C. Warren was a congressman for 20 years and Ocracoke was in his district. He became one of the leaders in our national House of Representatives and President Roosevelt appointed him Comptroller General of the United States, one of the most important offices in our land.

When the Hon. Mr. Warren arrives at Ocracoke—as he frequently does, because he loves the place—do the people roll out the red velvet carpet in his

77

honor? Are they impressed by the fact that such an important personage is visiting them?

Not so you could notice it.

In all my contacts with the people of Ocracoke I never have heard a single one of them refer to him as "Mr. Warren," either directly or indirectly. It's always: "Howdy, Lindsay; glad to see you," or some equally casual greeting. They regard him as being one of them and, needless to say, he appreciates it.

The same thing is true of Congressman Herbert Bonner who succeeded Mr. Warren in Congress. Everyone calls him "Herbert," either when referring to him or talking to him face to face.

Remember U. S. Senator Joseph Robinson from Arkansas; one of the outstanding figures in Congress for many years? Lindsay took him down to Ocracoke on a fishing trip many years ago and he wasn't there more than a day or so before Simey O'Neal, Bill Gaskill, Big Ike O'Neal and others were calling him "Joe" to his face.

And for heaven's sake, if you've never been to Ocracoke, don't make the mistake of patronizing the people down there just because they live in a location which might be described as being isolated. If you do, you're sunk, so far as the natives are concerned.

You may have all the money in the world, be known all over this country, wield all kinds of influence but it won't get you anywhere. If the people on the island like you it's because of you, yourself. If they don't like you, it's for the same reason.

The Wandering Ghost Ship

During the month of February, 1921, the five-masted schooner, *Carroll A. Deering*, was wrecked on the Outer Diamond Shoals, off the island of Hatteras. When the ship broke up under the constant beating of the waves, part of the hull floated toward shore and came to rest on the northern end of Ocracoke Island, about four miles south of Hatteras Inlet.

Sand gradually piled up over most of the hull, and you'd think this would be the end of the story, but it isn't.

The *Deering*, usually referred to as the ghost ship, refused to stay put in her grave of sand.

The year 1955 was a year of hurricanes—Connie, Dianne, Ione, etc. One of these caused the waves to undermine the old wreck. The sand was washed away from around it. An extra high tide lifted the old hull off the beach and pulled it out into deep water. Then it slowly drifted up the coast. It passed Hatteras Inlet. It sailed along for five or six miles farther and then it was washed ashore again, this time resting on the beach of Hatteras Island and thereby adding another chapter to the mysterious career of the *Carroll A. Deering*.

Remember, the wreck had occurred off Hatteras, which is part of Dare County. It drifted down to Ocracoke, which is part of Hyde County. By all rights it should have stayed there for the next hundred years or longer, but it didn't; it drifted right back to Dare County again.

Now for the story of this strange craft, leading up to the time when it was wrecked.

On the morning of February 18, 1921, the Coast Guardman in the tower of the station at Creeds Hill, near Cape Hatteras, squinted his eyes as he peered seaward and saw a five-masted schooner apparently just outside the treacherous Outer Diamond Shoals. He promptly notified the chief of the station that a ship seemed to be in trouble on the shoals. The men got busy and in a short while a surfboat put out to find out what was wrong. As the boat neared the big vessel, the men hailed her, but there was no answer. They shouted several times with the same result. Nor could anyone be seen aboard.

Some difficulty was encountered in making the surf-boat fast to the ship because there was a considerable sea running, but the feat was accomplished finally and the men clambered aboard.

From here on we'll let one of the men, James Midgett, tell the story in his own words:

"The minute my feet hit the deck I knew there was

something peculiar in the offing. We shouted two or three times more but again there was no answer. Then, from around the corner of the forward cabin there appeared a gray cat; just a plain, ordinary, every-day cat. She looked up at us and meowed. She kept right on meowing, and I reckon she was hungry. We then went below and searched the ship from stem to stern but couldn't find hide nor hair of any human being.

"Everything aboard was shipshape. The decks had been scrubbed clean and washed down. The hawsers were neatly coiled and there were no signs of any disorder or any indications of a hasty departure by the men aboard. The table in the mess-room was set with plates, knives and forks.

"We spent an hour aboard the vessel, looking into every closet and searching other places where a human being might be in hiding. In the forecastle we saw the crew's clothing, neatly stowed away. Same thing in the cabins of the captain and mates. Finally we got back into the surfboat again and returned to the station, taking the cat with us."

Official records of the Coast Guard contain the same story in somewhat more lengthy detail.

The next storm that came up after the *Deering* went aground broke the ship in two, but she still remained above water. About a year later, a Coast Guard cutter out of Norfolk dynamited the derelict because it was considered a menace to navigation. Part of the wreck drifted ashore on Ocracoke Island. For a year or more the stern and bow remained in plain view, but slowly most of the wreck was covered with sand and there she stayed until 1955, when she resumed her travelings once more.

Of course there were all sorts of explanations offered in connection with the deserted ship. Some thought that maybe the officers and crew had been stricken with some kind of plague. When a man would die, the others would throw him overboard. Maybe the last man disposed of himself in the same manner. Others guessed that the ship was attacked by pirates and the men aboard were either captured or killed. In contradiction of this explanation, it is pointed out that there were no signs of any violence whatsoever. Everything was in order.

Still others surmised that there might have been a mutiny and the officers were killed. The crew got scared and sailed off in the ship's boat, landing somewhere along the coast and then dispersing.

I talked to Big Ike O'Neal about it a few months before he died ten years ago. Ike said, "My idea ain't quite as sensational as that expressed by some other people. I believe that when the *Deering* ran aground, the captain and crew got panicky. They were afraid she was going to break up in a hurry and they'd be drowned in the rough water. So they got aboard the ship's boat with the intention of heading for shore and safety. But the water gets mighty rough on the outer shoal. I believe that the boat capsized before it got very far and everybody was drowned. However, that's just my idea and it, too, may be wrong."

It may be wrong but it certainly sounds logical. However, nobody knows exactly what did take place, and chances are that nobody ever will. The *Deering* grounded more than forty years ago and if the mystery hasn't been solved by now, there isn't much hope of its ever being solved.

The designation of "ghost ship" seems to be well deserved, particularly in view of what happened last year when she decided to change her last resting place and move farther up the coast.

Farthest North Palm

This palm tree grew in the front yard of Mr. and Mrs. Floyd Styron and, so far as I know, it was the most northerly palm tree anywhere along the Atlantic coast. There may be one or two smaller ones farther north, but nothing as large as this one. A storm came along recently and ruined it.

Here's how the tree came to be there:

A long time ago, one of the Styron boys was selling the *Pennsylvania Grit*, a weekly publication popular a couple of generations ago. He proved to be an excellent salesman and won a prize.

The prize was the palm tree. It was just a little shoot when it arrived but it has done extremely well by itself.

Suppose You Got Sick?

From time to time I've heard people say: "I'd be rather scared to go down to Ocracoke and spend very much time there."

"Why?"

"Because there's no doctor on the island. What in the world would happen to you if you were suddenly taken ill? You could die half a dozen times before a doctor could get to you or before you could get to a doctor."

That's not quite an accurate statement.

Here's what happens when someone on the island becomes ill:

First, a member of the family or a neighbor will run over to several of the places where visitors stay and will endeavor to ascertain whether a doctor is among them.

Let's say that no doctor shows up.

Second, word would be sent to Miss Kathleen Bragg or to Mrs. Elsie Garrish, wife of Irving. They are two registered trained nurses and are residents of

86

Ocracoke. Miss Bragg is a graduate of the nursing school at the Rocky Mount Hospital, and Mrs. Garrish received her training at the Rex Hospital in Raleigh.

Either of them would be pretty apt to know what was wrong with the patient. If the condition wasn't too serious, the Coast Guard would be notified. The patient would be placed aboard a boat and rushed to the new hospital at Sea Level, two miles south of Atlantic.

But suppose an operation was required immediately —what then?

Once again someone would hurry to the Coast Guard and describe the condition of the patient. A Coast Guardman would then call up the duty officer at district headquarters in Norfolk, giving full details. A helicopter would be ordered out of Elizabeth City with a doctor aboard, if his presence were badly needed. Also any medicines that might be required. The helicopter would take the patient aboard and carry him or her to Sea Level in about twenty minutes. Or perhaps to Morehead City, the Marine Hospital in Norfolk or the new hospital in Washington.

This has happened on several occasions, but they have been few and far between. It all goes to show, however, that a person on Ocracoke, taken critically ill, could be taken to a hospital just about as quickly as many people living in rural areas on the mainland.

And then, too, there's this other point to be taken into consideration. People on Ocracoke just don't get sick as often as do the people on the mainland. They've got very little to make them sick. They eat plain, substantial food, they live well-regulated lives, they don't dissipate and they enjoy a fine climate.

I've talked to a number of Ocracokers who have told me that they never have had a sick day since they were born.

There undoubtedly are several contributing factors to this: the way they live—regular habits and plain substantial food—being out in the fresh air practically all day long, and not being tied down to the many sedentary jobs one finds on the mainland.

Swing Your Partners!

At one time, square dancing was as much a part of life on Ocracoke as fishing. Old and young alike participated in this form of recreation and they had it down to a science so far as perfect rhythm was concerned.

But today, although you'll see an occasional square dance, jitterbugging is the order of the day—and it's enough to make a mature, native-born Ocracoker disgusted with the world as a whole.

But here's how things were carried on until recent years. I found these facts in an article I wrote up about Ocracoke fifteen years ago.

There's usually a dance on Saturday nights and, sometimes on special occasions, during the middle of the week.

When there's something extra special going on—like the Fourth of July celebration—a small, three-piece orchestra supplies the music. It consists of guitar, banjo and fiddle. Mostly, however, a juke box is used. It has in its repertoire many hill-billy tunes suitable as an accompaniment for square dancing. The records don't take long to play. While the machine is switching

them around, the dancers stop in their tracks and hold their positions. As soon as the music blares forth again, off they go with whatever figure they were dancing when the previous record ended.

As a general thing, the dances are supposed to start

at eight o'clock, but it always takes the participants a little while to get started. They'll sit around, talking to one another. A good many of the boys remain outside of the building, apparently not interested in what is going on inside. Occasionally, during this interim, the girls dance with one another. And then, as though acting on a given signal, everybody gets out on the floor and the square dance is under way.

Done properly, it's just about as pretty, graceful and fascinating a sight as you ever have seen on a dance floor. The people of Ocracoke learned the figures when they were youngsters. It isn't unusual to see men and women, fifty or sixty years old, take part in the dance and never miss a lick. Not only that, but they're just as lively and adept as the younger ones.

There are several men who are experts at calling the figures. Each of these callers has one or two specialties of his own which are mingled with the general run of maneuvers.

"Balance off!" comes the cry. This is the signal for the dancers to stand around in a big circle preparatory to starting the dance.

"Promenade!" Off they go, turning to the right and proceeding with a kind of shuffling gait, partners moving along with their hands crossed.

"Ladies to the right, men to the left!" They go around the circle in opposite directions: ladies straight ahead, men in reverse.

Then come a number of other calls:

"Dance the star!"

"Dive for the oyster!"

"Dance by fours!"

"Bird in the cage!"

And so on, some of the movements being of an extremely intricate nature. But never a mis-step or sign of faltering. Everyone on the floor knows what he or she is supposed to do, and they do it. The only time there's any confusion is when some visitors from the mainland get the idea that they are square dancers and inject themselves into the figure.

They can get things balled up in a hurry.

On the other hand, there are some visitors who have been going to Ocracoke ever since they were young and they're just about as good as the natives. They're from Washington, Swan Quarter, Beaufort and other places in the coastal area.

It takes about fifteen minutes to run through a square dance. Then the dancers rest for a bit while the juke box plays music suitable for the one-step, or "round dance" as it is better known. Those who are timid about taking part in the square dance do a little stepping on their own account before the next set is called.

Soon the voice of the announcer is heard again: "Balance off!" And away they go.

When you go to a dance at your country club you may attend a cocktail party first, arriving at the club at about eleven o'clock and dancing until two or three in the morning.

Not so at Ocracoke. The crowd gathers at the recreation hall at about eight o'clock. Admission price is a quarter. The dance is over by eleven o'clock, in time for everyone to get a good night's sleep.

Drinking? Yes, there's some. You'll find some of the young men taking a drink on the outside of the building but it very, very seldom becomes objectionable in any way, so nobody pays any attention to it.

93

Law and Order

Suppose you woke up one night while at Ocracoke and found a man in your room, rifling your possessions on the dresser, or making a search through your apparel, what would you do?

Would you stick your head out of the window and holler, "Police! Help, Police!"

It wouldn't do much good because the nearest policeman to Ocracoke is at Atlantic, thirty miles away by water. To tell the truth, I'm not exactly sure that Atlantic has a policeman either.

However, all this is purely hypothetical because there is a mighty slim chance of anyone being in your room and trying to rob you.

No burglar, if he has good sense, would try to practice his profession on Ocracoke Island, and here's why:

Suppose he broke open the safe in the Community Store and got away with a couple of hundred dollars, where could he go? He'd either have to do a tall piece of swimming or else he'd take his departure in a boat. In either event, the Coast Guard, with a faster boat, would soon be on his trail. And so, perhaps, would a helicopter or two.

No, there are no burglars on Ocracoke. People in the village never bother about locks and keys in their doors. I doubt whether there is a single resident who ever thinks of locking his doors and windows at night or while he is away from home overnight. As a matter of fact, I heard of one couple that went to visit relatives in St. Louis and were away about three weeks.

They left their house open the entire time.

I mentioned something about this to Wahab Howard one day. "I've lived here all my life," he said, "and I don't believe I ever have heard of a single robbery, or any other kind of crime, for that matter. Sometimes some of the fellows will get a little too much liquor aboard, and there may be a little fist swinging, but aside from something of that nature, we never have any trouble on the island."

As for visitors, they're vacationists, fishermen and hunters. They're hardly the type who would break into people's houses or commit some other kind of crime.

Ocracokers are law-abiding people and this may be due to the fact that there is no visible evidence of law enforcement agencies anywhere. There's no police department. The sheriff and his deputies are at Swan Quarter, on the mainland.

No policemen, no patrolmen, nobody stepping around with a gun swinging from his hip, no jail and no courts. And the reason for this is that there's no earthly use for them on Ocracoke.

Sport Fishing

In trying to bring you information on this subject I might just as well be frank and candid. When it comes to sport fishing I know just about nothing.

I quit going fishing a long time ago because of the same thing happening on every trip.

Friends invite me to go with them in a boat out from Morehead City, Wrightsville, Ocracoke or some other place along the coast. We arrive at a point which the captain tells us is an excellent spot. He says we're bound to catch plenty of fish, so we get our tackle ready and cast our lines overboard.

And you know what happens?

Here's what happens: not a single, solitary fish!

It seems, however, that there always is a logical explanation for this. Actually there are four:

1. The wind isn't right.
2. The tide isn't right.
3. The water is too hot or cold.
4. The weather is cloudy or else the sun is shining.

This has happened time and again. The remarkable thing about it is that this same boat with the same

people aboard, excepting me, can go out the following day and catch enough fish to founder the craft.

Maybe it's my fault. Regardless of whether it is or not, I became disgusted a long time ago and haven't been fishing in years.

Perhaps I'm like Congressman Herbert Bonner.

Herbert and a friend were fishing in the Pungo River. An elderly Negro, Uncle Mose, was paddling the boat for them. The fish weren't biting and Herbert became impatient. He directed Uncle Mose to paddle to another location. Still no fish. This went on most of the afternoon. Uncle Mose at last got slightly impatient also. After having been directed to paddle here, there and yonder, he gave a deep sigh, accompanied by a discouraging shake of the head. "Mr. Bonner," he said, "I'll oar her wherever you wants me to, but it won't make any difference. Mr. Bonner, you aire a sorry fisherman."

That describes me exactly. Fish and I are decidedly allergic to each other.

No, I'm no fisherman, but a book about Ocracoke most certainly would be incomplete if there wasn't something in it about fishing in the waters surrounding the island, so I'll do the best I can.

One of the most sought-after fish by sportsmen who visit Ocracoke is the channel bass, better known locally as the drum. They range in weight from a few pounds to seventy-five. I believe the record fish caught up to now weighed 82 pounds. Large numbers are brought in every year weighing forty, fifty and sixty pounds.

It used to be that most of the drum were caught from boats in the sound, but in recent years fishermen have been favoring surf casting on the ocean side of the island. In the spring of the year, however, quite a number of fishermen still prefer the boats.

There are several so-called party boats in Silver

Lake and you won't have any difficulty in chartering one of these craft.

If you want to go surf casting, you make a date with Jake's or Wilbur's taxicab service. They'll call for you at the hotel and will drive you over to the beach. You'd better rely on them to pick out a fishing spot for you, instead of depending on your own judgment, because they have had plenty of experience.

They'll leave you there with your fishing tackle and a jug of water and will pick you up whenever you tell them to. If you get tired before the designated hour, it won't do you any good to decide to quit, because they won't show up until they're supposed to.

If you haven't been out in the sun very much it also might be a good idea to carry along an umbrella. The sun can get mighty hot on the beach, and it can ruin your entire vacation if you're not careful.

In the spring the biggest run of drum occurs about the middle of April and continues through the end of May. In the fall it's September through November. Fishermen come every year from New York, Philadelphia, Baltimore, Cleveland and other distant places as well as from many towns in North Carolina.

In May the sport fishermen also catch plenty of trout or weakfish, kingfish, whiting or sea mullets, and bluefish. In the summer and fall a goodly number of pompanos also are caught, as are a general assortment of other fish. Some of the visiting fishermen like to wade in the waters of Pamlico Sound at night and spear flounders. It's a lot of fun, enjoyed by men and women alike.

For the most part, the boats confine themselves to the waters of Pamlico Sound, although they also will anchor off Point-o'-Beach in Ocracoke Inlet.

Trolling for blues and mackerel is popular. During June and continuing until the middle of July, quite a number of cobia are brought in. This is an excellent game fish and some have been caught weighing sixty, seventy and even eighty pounds. The average is between 20 and 30 pounds.

Sheepshead also are caught in the sound.

There isn't very much fishing done in the Atlantic. The principal reason for this is that Ocracokers have a healthy respect for the ocean. Sometimes a captain will take his boat out to sea if the skipper in another craft will accompany him, but otherwise there's nothing doing. The boatmen on Ocracoke Island have had too much experience with the ocean to play around in it.

As a general thing, fishing is good at Ocracoke and that's why so many visitors come back year after year. I've looked back over some of the hotel registers and have found the same names a dozen or more times.

When I say that fishing is good I may be making an understatement because I believe it is generally agreed that there is no finer place along the entire Atlantic coast for engaging in this sport than Ocracoke.

The Wild Ponies

Anyone who ever has heard of Ocracoke has heard of the wild ponies that roam along the outer banks.

Don't get the wrong idea in connection with the word "pony." These horses are larger than Shetland ponies but they're somewhat smaller than the average-sized horse. Just about the size of polo ponies. As a matter of fact, Ocracoke horses are greatly in demand as polo ponies.

Their origin is uncertain. The story I've been hearing for many years is that a ship was wrecked off Ocracoke Island a hundred or more years ago with several Arabian horses aboard. These animals managed to reach shore safely. They took refuge in the wooded area of the island and gradually increased in number.

There aren't nearly as many ponies on Ocracoke today as there were ten, fifteen or twenty years ago. And there used to be wild cows, but all of these have been removed. Here's a description of these animals and events connected with them as things used to be.

How about drinking water? They provide their own

drinking water in a rather unusual manner. You may not believe this but it's the truth and if you're ever riding or walking about the island you may see it for yourself. Here's what happens:

When the horses get good and thirsty they start digging in the sand with their front hooves. They dig down a couple of feet or so and strike fresh water. Then they proceed to drink their fill.

If you think that sounds fishy, listen to this:

There also are wild cows on the island. These animals take care of themselves, just as the horses do. They roam at large and eat grass and leaves. When it comes to digging for water, however, they're up against it because they can't use their front legs the way horses do.

So what happens?

Simply this: they hang around and watch the horses. When the horses dig water holes the cows wait for them to get through drinking. Then the cows amble up to the hole and slake their own thirst.

One of the most widely publicised events on Ocracoke is the annual pony penning. This takes place on the Fourth of July and always attracts a large number of visitors to the island.

Late on the night of July 3, five or six men, riding on ponies, leave the village and head for the northern tip of the island. They ride about three hours and then put up in a cabin and spend the night. The next morning they're up at daybreak and, after a bite to eat, mount their horses and proceed to head in a southerly direction.

For the most part the ponies are fairly tractable. With the exception of the young colts they've been through this same experience before and are used to it.

But occasionally some of the horses become balky. They head for the waters of Pamlico Sound and wade out as far as they can—sometimes half a mile or so. One or more of the riders have to follow. Eventually the horses are headed toward the island again and join the others.

The animals approach the village near the Coast Guard station. They thunder along the narrow pavement until they come to the pen which has been built on the shore of Silver Lake near the inn. Amidst much confusion they are herded into the pen and the gate is closed.

The primary purpose of the penning is to brand the colts that have been foaled during the past year. I was somewhat puzzled as to how the colts could be identified as to ownership but the explanation is simple. The young animals never leave their mothers. When a man sees a colt sticking close to the side of one of his mares he knows the little fellow belongs to him.

The youngsters are branded before being turned loose again.

Sometimes there are one or more purchasers who desire to buy some of the horses. Otherwise, after having been kept in the pen a couple of hours or so— time enough for everybody to get a good look at them —the ponies are given their freedom and immediately scatter all over the island.

That's how things used to be. In recent years the pony pennings haven't been as big events as they formerly were, due principally to the fact that there aren't as many ponies as there used to be.

Hospitality in Reverse

Ocracokers are hospitable and friendly people. When they get to know you, they'll do anything in the world for you.

After your third, fourth or fifth visit to the island you'll begin to get fairly well acquainted with some of the citizens: you'll recognize them when you meet them and be able to call them by name.

All of which adds to the enjoyment of your visit.

But you should see what happens when an Ocracoker goes to the mainland and runs into some of the people who have been on the island!

Having lived in Washington and New Bern for a number of years, I've seen what takes place.

Here's an illustration:

Ben O'Neal arrives in Washington to attend to some business matters. He walks down Main Street. Every few paces he is stopped by people who want to shake hands with him. He is invited into the drugstore for a Coke or, if it's late in the afternoon, he is invited to someone's home to partake of something a little stronger. Men, women and children stop to speak to him. Half a dozen or more people urge him to spend the night at their homes. There is sincerity in the friendliness of their greeting.

The late Big Ike O'Neal told me one day in Washington, "I always feel like a big shot when I come here, and it sure is a mighty fine feeling."

There's something rather unusual about this. When a resident from Greenville, Williamston, New Bern or Farmville appears on the streets of Washington—and he happens to be someone you know—there is a brief, friendly greeting, but that's all. When an Ocracoker appears on the scene, his presence brings about almost an ovation.

The farther he gets away from home, the more cordial is the welcome he gets.

In looking over the hotel registers, I've seen names of quite a number of visitors from Cleveland, Ohio. I'd be willing to bet that if Thurston Gaskill were to go out to Cleveland, the folks whom he had taken fishing in Pamlico Sound would welcome him with a brass band, accompanied by the entire baseball team of the Cleveland Indians.

If the Governor of North Carolina and Charlie McWilliams were to appear on the streets of Beaufort, there is no question in my mind as to who would get the heartier greeting.

It'd be Charlie.

Berkley Manor

For the most part, the homes of the people on Ocracoke Island follow the same pattern of architecture. They're frame structures, one or two stories. Nothing fancy about them, just nice, comfortable homes.

Exceptions to the rule are a couple of residences built by Sam Jones of Norfolk.

Sam was born in Swan Quarter, in same county as Ocracoke. He made a lot of money up in Norfolk. The houses at Ocracoke were built about twelve years ago for himself and sons. The latest, shown above, is particularly. outstanding. It has 32 dormer windows and sixteen rooms. It was completed in the early part of 1955.

107

Old Quawk's Day

Prior to writing this book I went to Carleton Kelly's house after supper and, during the course of our conversation, I said something about Zack Bacon wanting to go fishing the following day.

Zack had accompanied me on the trip to Ocracoke.

"Surf fishing?" inquired Carleton.

"No, I believe he wants to go in a boat. Do you think Thurston Gaskill or some of the boys would be able to take him out tomorrow morning?"

"They might be able to go but I doubt whether they will," he replied.

"Why?"

"Old Quawk's Day, you know."

I didn't know, so naturally this brought about another question and it, in turn, resulted in an explanation of the meaning of Old Quawk's Day.

Old salts on Ocracoke, and elsewhere on the outer banks, hesitate a long time before they'll go out in a boat on March 16. Sudden squalls are said to be almost certain to appear, menacing the safety of large and small craft. Quite a number of boats have been in

difficulty on this particular day, according to stories I've heard, and several lives have been lost.

Old Quawk was a blasphemous West Indian half-breed. A ship was wrecked off the outer banks near the village of Ocracoke and he was washed ashore, more dead than alive. He was revived, regained his health and decided to remain on the island.

This happened during the early part of the last century.

Quawk was a disagreeable, unfriendly, surly in-dividual. He looked like you imagine a cut-throat pirate would look, and there were some people on the island who thought that he had been one while living in the Caribbean. Quawk didn't deny it. On the contrary it seemed to please him to try and convince everyone that he was an extremely tough character.

What his real name was, no one ever found out. It wasn't long after the wreck, however, before he was given the name by which he was to be known there-after—Old Quawk. The natives agreed that his voice, particularly when he was excited or under a strain, sounded very much like the shrill cry of the night heron, known locally as a "quawk."

One day the fishermen found that high winds and stormy seas would keep them ashore. They feared for their unattended fish nets out in Pamlico Sound and they stood a good chance of suffering heavy financial loss as a result of weather conditions.

None of them was daring enough to set sail into the waters of the sound.

With Old Quawk it was different. He, too, feared

for his nets and was determined to go out and attend to them. Shouting angry oaths into the teeth of the gale, he untied his small sailboat and nosed it from its mooring place.

Other fishermen sought to restrain him from his foolhardy action but he paid no heed. He defied God to do His worst. His cursing caused those within hearing range to shudder. Old Quawk yelled at them, calling them cowards and weaklings.

His boat moved quickly away from the cove. Soon it disappeared from sight. Not only that, but it disappeared for good, for nothing was heard of Old Quawk after that. And nothing was seen of his boat.

Ever since that event took place, March 16 has been regarded as a dangerous day for leaving the safe waters of the various little bays near the village. It is a day to be spent in port and not out in a boat.

Today the story of Old Quawk usually is told with a smile, and nobody pretends to believe it except those inclined to be extra superstitious. Still, March 16 comes during the stormy time of the year and it isn't a date that might be termed propitious for fishing.

Zack made some inquiries the next morning but he didn't have any success in getting a captain to agree to take him out into the waters of the sound.

The Picture Show

The moving picture theatre, which occupies the southern wing of the Wahab Village Hotel, isn't making anyone rich.

Shows are run on Tuesday and Saturday nights. Admission is 40 cents for adults, 25 cents for children. Seating capacity is around 250.

There's nothing fancy about interior decorations.

C. F. Boyette, manager of the hotel, is also manager of the theatre. He's not optimistic about the future of the business and says he'd be just as well satisfied if the shows were discontinued altogether.

The film costs $16.50. Then there's the cost of postage, wages for a machine operator, lights and power, etc. Boyette figures that the total cost involved in producing one show is $30.

Now then, let's see. Take 40 adults at 40 cents ($16.00) and 60 children at 25 cents ($15.00) and you have only $31.00 in revenue.

That's about the average attendance. Sometimes the crowd is larger than that but there are other occasions when it is much smaller.

"There have been times," Boyette told me, "when we have had only a dozen people in the theatre."

Westerns are the most popular type of movies, and the kids applaud vigorously when the hero triumphs over the villain. The folksy, down-to-earth kind also are well received. Pictures like *The Barefooted Contessa* don't make much of an impression. When a film of that type appears on the screen, the kids usually start laughing and talking among themselves.

If you want an opportunity for making a lot of money, I suggest you pass up any plan you may have in mind for operating a picture show at Ocracoke at the present time.

How Jim Baugham Gaskill Came Home

James Baugham Gaskill was the son of Captain and Mrs. Bill Gaskill who for many years operated Pamlico Inn on Ocracoke Island.

I recall Jim when he was a youngster of six or seven years. A quiet and rather shy boy who enjoyed being by himself, fishing or digging clams in the sound close to Pamlico Inn.

Shortly before World War II he joined the U. S. Government Engineers. Later he became a member of the Merchant Marine and, during the war, was second mate aboard the steamer, *Caribsea*.

The *Caribsea* was a cargo ship, sailing up and down the eastern coast. On this particular trip she was heading north, bound for Norfolk.

She was a rather slow craft. It was night when she passed Cape Lookout. Jim, who had been on duty on the bridge, announced he was going to bed.

"Aren't you going to wait until you see Ocracoke light?" asked a fellow officer.

"No," said Jim, "I'm tired and I'm going to turn in. I've seen that beacon too many times to stay awake and look for it."

It was about four hours later that a German submarine fired a torpedo at the *Caribsea*. It was a devastatingly accurate shot. A big hole was made in one side of the vessel right at the waterline. She sank in a matter of a minute or two. There were only five survivors—those who were on the bridge and on deck when the torpedo struck. The ones below, including Jim Baugham, didn't have a chance. They went down with the ship.

Three days after the sinking of the *Caribsea*, Chris Gaskill was walking along the beach on the lower part of Ocracoke Island. Chris was a cousin of Jim's. He observed something being washed ashore a short distance ahead of him. Picking it up he saw it was a framed certificate, made out to his cousin, Jim, second mate of the ship, *Caribsea*. He took it back to the village with him and showed it to members of the family and other residents on the island.

The following day something else appeared—a spar which had *Caribsea* painted on it. The certificate had been found on the ocean side of the island; the spar had drifted through Ocracoke Inlet and came ashore at the breakwater right where Pamlico Inn used to be located and where Jim Baugham had been born and reared.

Homer Howard took the spar and had a cross made of it. This cross may now be seen on the altar of the Methodist Church.

Only One Colored Family

In recent years there has been only one Negro family on Ocracoke; Leonard Randolph Bryant and his wife, Jane. They passed away a few years ago. They had nine children but only three are living on the island today.

Leonard was born at Engelhard, Hyde County, in 1896. Jane's parents came to Ocracoke two years before the Civil War. Here's a description of their life on the island as it appeared in a newspaper article published in 1960:

There has been quite a stir about segregation in various parts of the country. You know all about that so there's no use in going into it here. But let's see what the attitude about this is on Ocracoke.

Leonard and Jane have a house of their own. It doesn't take much money for them to live comfortably. He does carpentry work and other odd jobs and also a little fishing. White folks live all around them.

If Leonard wants to see Ike O'Neal about something, he'll go around to Ike's house.

"Come on in the house, Leonard."

117

They sit out on the porch or in the living room.

Maybe Ike's daughter, Mrs. Jesse Garrish, will join them and say, "Papa, don't you and Leonard want a glass of lemonade?"

The lemonade is served and drunk.

Everything is perfectly natural and there is nothing strained about the situation.

The same is true with respect to Jane. She visits with the women on the island and they visit with her, discussing household matters or watching television.

Leonard and Jane attend the Methodist Church regularly. They usually sit in the rear, not because they have been requested to do so but because that's what they want to do.

They join other members of the church in communion, waiting until the rest of the congregation has participated before going forward. Not because anyone has directed them to do this; they do it of their own volition.

Leonard served as sexton of the church for many years. He always wore a white coat, greeted the members cordially as they entered the building, showed visitors to their seats, passed out the hymnals and attended to the bell ringing. He's getting rather old now, so he has abandoned most of these duties, but he still is a regular communicant.

Julius is the only one of the children with whom I am personally acquainted. He's about twenty-five years old. As a child, he and his brothers and sisters played with the white children on the island. They did not attend school with other children but at one time the teachers heard the lessons of the Negro children after the regular daily session had been brought to a close. For the most part, however, Jane took her youngsters to the mainland, to Beaufort County, where they obtained their education.

At the pony penning festival every Fourth of July, a beauty queen is selected. She rides in the parade on a truck and inside a veiled-in enclosure. When the veil is removed, there sits Jane, peeling potatoes, eating watermelon or engaged in some other ordinary chore.

Everybody gets a big kick out of this, especially Jane.

Said old Leonard to me recently, "There ain't no finer people anywhere than the people of Ocracoke. They always have been mighty good to me and my family. I never been sorry that I came here to live."

119

Burial Associations and Funerals

Burial associations are nothing new and have been in operation in all parts of the country for many years. All of them are run in practically the same manner. Members are assessed a certain amount which is paid in the form of monthly dues. And then, when a death occurs, the association takes care of all burial expenses.

In North Carolina all this business is supervised by the State Burial Commission with headquarters in Raleigh.

Down on Ocracoke there's a burial association which does not come under the supervision of the State Commission. It is not operated by any undertaker or funeral home because there are no undertakers or funeral homes. There are no monthly dues. It's a community proposition entirely.

An annual meeting is held at which officers are elected. The actual dues are ten cents a year. This is used to pay for stationery, stamps and other expenses incidental to keeping records. Practically everybody on the island belongs to the association.

When a member dies it means that all the other members have to pay a quarter. The secretary of the association holds office hours on the following three Wednesdays and the members go to him and pay their assessments. If they don't pay by the third Wednesday, they are dropped from the roll. In the event they want to rejoin later on, they're assessed an additional ten cents.

I was told it is seldom that there is any trouble collecting the assessments following a death on the island.

Sometimes two or three months pass by without any assessment; at other times they are quite frequent.

The association has operated for many years, without any regular payment of dues, and the system apparently has proved to be satisfactory to all concerned.

With reference to funerals, I'd be willing to bet that there are mighty few places in North Carolina where a funeral is attended by so many relatives as is the case on Ocracoke. There's been quite a lot of intermarriage among residents of the island. Not only that but their comparative isolation and close community interests have combined to make them a clannish people in many respects.

When a person passes away, friends of the family go around and make arrangements for a choir to sing at the services. They also select the hymns to be sung, and help shroud the corpse. Then they go around to the

Community Store and buy a coffin.

There usually are four coffins kept at the store. As soon as one is used, Jesse Garrish orders another one from Washington. In this manner the stock is kept up constantly.

The casket is carried to the home of the deceased on a truck. Most funerals in the past have been held from the residence but there has been somewhat of a change lately and the present trend is to have the services held from the church.

All burial services take place within 24 hours after death occurs because there's no embalming done on the island.

Relatives living away from the island are notified. Flowers are ordered from Beaufort or Morehead City. These are brought in by the ferry if there is time; otherwise, Jesse Taylor, who operates the airport at Beaufort, flies them in.

When flowers are in season some folks make their own wreaths.

The pallbearers are relatives. Everyone quits work during the hour of the funeral. The stores and other places of business are closed. Those who can get inside the house proceed to do so, but most of the men stand outside while the services are in progress.

A couple of hymns are sung and then everyone views the body for the last time while the singing continues. Used to be that the pallbearers would carry the body to the family burial ground, with friends and relatives following. Now, however, inasmuch as the community cemetery is coming more and more into use, the casket is placed on a truck and the mourners follow in jeeps, trucks or on foot.

The casket is placed in a box and lowered into the grave. Everyone remains while the pallbearers fill the grave, make a mound thereon, place a slab of wood at either end and then cover the mound with flowers.

There's something about the simplicity of a funeral at Ocracoke that makes it very impressive.

The Civic Club

Cities and towns everywhere pride themselves on their civic clubs—chambers of commerce, merchants associations, Rotary, Kiwanis and so on. And rightfully so, because these organizations do some mighty fine work as a rule.

Up until about ten years ago, Ocracoke didn't have anything of this nature. The women had their church societies and their P.T.A., but the men were completely clubless.

They decided that something should be done about the matter.

Among the leaders in the movement were Theodore Rondthaler and Captain Peele. They talked to others and found support for a movement to organize a civic club. A meeting was held in the schoolhouse, officers were elected, by-laws were adopted and the club was ready to function.

The name was to be the Civic Club. It has been operating very nicely and undoubtedly will continue to do so because all of the members are intensely interested in it.

Here's an account of a typical meeting I attended a month or so before writing this book:

A committee of five men had been appointed to attend to arrangements. They were Sid Tolson, Rev. W. R. Hale, Jack Thompson, Henry Wilder and Sam Brooks. Their job was to cook supper and have it ready when the club assembled at the schoolhouse at 7:30.

Thirty-nine members were in attendance. Supper consisted of oyster stew, crackers, pickles and coffee. And if you think that oyster stew doesn't make a filling meal, you've never eaten the kind of stew that they serve on Ocracoke.

After supper the regular business session was held.

Minutes of the previous meeting were read and approved.

The treasurer read his report which showed that the club had a balance of $28.85 on hand. (The dues, incidentally, are 50 cents a month.)

There was a discussion relative to getting some new booklets printed, publicizing Ocracoke.

Thurston Gaskill urged that the club sponsor an oyster planting project. Osyters have been getting rather scarce in that area and Thurston felt that something should be done about it.

The club gave its endorsement.

A letter was read from a retiring missionary, wanting to know about Ocracoke with a view of making his home there. The secretary was instructed to communicate with him.

Inasmuch as funds in the treasury were getting

rather low, it was moved, seconded and carried that from now on the club wouldn't buy a wreath every time there was a death in the family of a member. Instead, members were asked to donate 10 cents each, voluntarily.

A few of the members were behind in their dues and the secretary was notified to get after them and see whether or not the money could be collected.

It was decided to invite the Boy and Cub Scouts to the next meeting. Captain Westcott and Captain Midgett of the Coast Guard said they would furnish the turkeys and cook them.

A committee was appointed to co-operate with the Park Service in connection with erosion just north of the Coast Guard station where it is planned to make a park. It was pointed out that the best solution would be the construction of a jetty. A committee was named to look after this.

Mr. Brooks of the Park Service showed slides of the Petrified Forest, after which the club adjourned.

The Business of Shrimping

Shrimping is a business which has its ups and downs. Today, most of the Ocracokers who used to earn their living by going out after shrimp have turned their attention to other pursuits that provide a more steady income.

However, it's an interesting vocation and perhaps you might be interested in a few details.

A typical shrimping boat is 40 feet in length. The crew usually consists of a captain and two men. The boat will leave its dock on Silver Lake at about four o'clock in the morning and will head in the direction of Bluff Shoal Lighthouse out in Pamlico Sound.

First thing to be done is to heave the try net overboard. This net measures from 6 to 8 feet in length and is dragged along the bottom while the boat moves along slowly at about three miles per hour. It requires only one line or cable.

The net is dragged along for five or ten minutes. Then it is pulled up. If there are as many as 10 to 15 shrimp in it, that's a good sign. In order to make sure,

however, it may be tried out once or twice more. If the showing of shrimp is still good, then the big net goes overboard. At a somewhat accelerated speed the big net is dragged for about one and one-half hours. In the meantime the try net is kept overboard also, being hauled up frequently in order to check on the shrimp.

After the hour and one-half is up, the big net is hauled up by means of a winch supplemented by manual labor. If the try net hasn't lied there'll be plenty of shrimp in the haul, along with seaweed, turtles, crabs, mullets, croakers, oysters and so on. Nothing interests the fishermen except the shrimp; all the other stuff is thrown overboard.

The men put on their oilskins and gloves when the big net is hauled in. If they didn't, they'd soon be drenched to the skin as a result of the slime being thrown around by the threshing fish.

If the haul yields as much as 75 pounds, the men are satisfied. They sell the shrimp at prices ranging from 25 to 35 cents a pound.

There are a number of empty boxes aboard. These are iced and the shrimp are thrown in. The dealer—the man who buys the shrimp—furnishes both ice and boxes.

Small boats come back into port at the end of the day. Larger craft will spend one or more nights in the sound, depending on what kind of luck they have. In flying across Pamlico Sound from the mainland to Ocracoke I've seen as many as a hundred shrimpers hard at work.

Shrimping is done on shares. On a two-man boat—captain and mate—the money is split three ways: the boat gets a third, the captain gets a third and the mate gets a third. The division is made after actual operating expenses have been deducted; food, gasoline, oil, etc.

The shrimping season starts about May 10, although the date varies as much as a week or two either way. It customarily lasts until the last of June. Shrimp caught in the spring are spotted; each has a spot near the end of the tail and they are of medium size.

Summer shrimp are the real big ones, known as jumbos.

Fall shrimp are known as green-tail shrimp. They, too, are jumbos, but not quite as large as the ones caught during hot weather.

Most of the shrimp are caught in the sound. Twice a year, however, the boats will sail through the inlet and drag their nets in the ocean. This occurs when the shrimp are coming into the sound in the spring and again when they go back into the ocean during the fall.

At times a lot of money can be made shrimping; at other times it can be a back-breaking, unprofitable task.

"How much money does a man make at this business?" I asked Willie Bryan Hunnings, who had been shrimping several years.

"That's like asking how much money does a man make shooting craps," he replied. "You just naturally can't tell. One week may be good and then you may have a month of bad luck."

"What's the most you've ever heard of anyone making?"

"Well, two years ago Travis Williams took in $1,000 during the course of a week."

Willie Bryan thought for a moment and then added: "Those kind of weeks don't come very often."

Died Before He Was Born

Captain Steve Basnight, who used to be chief of the Coast Guard station on the island a number of years ago, gazed at me triumphantly as we stood in one of the many small graveyards in the village.

"Now do you believe it?" he demanded. "Or do you still think that I made up the story?"

We were looking at the tombstone over the grave of Warren Wahab. The inscription stated that he had been born in 1855 and had died in 1842.

That, of course, was an impossibility even on Ocracoke where all kinds of unusual things have happened since the first white man settled there. I said as much to Captain Steve.

"All I know is what the inscription says," he retorted.

Here's the explanation, according to my way of thinking:

Relatives of Warren Wahab placed an order for the tombstone and had it made in Washington, New Bern

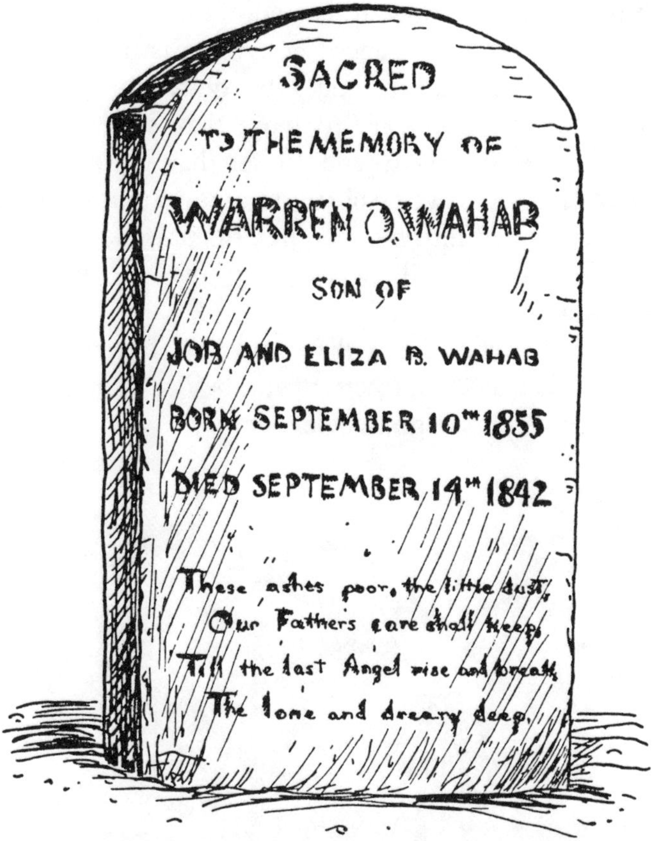

SACRED

TO THE MEMORY OF

WARREN O. WAHAB

SON OF

JOB AND ELIZA B. WAHAB

BORN SEPTEMBER 10th 1855

DIED SEPTEMBER 14th 1842

These ashes poor, the little dust,
Our Fathers care shall keep,
Till the last Angel rise and break,
The lone and dreary deep.

or some other town along the coast. The man who cut the stone either was careless with his figures or else they hadn't been written very distinctly. When the stone arrived at Ocracoke, the probabilities are that the error was discovered immediately. But it would have taken such a long time to get another stone that the family decided to put up this one and have it altered at a later and more convenient date.

But you know how it is about things like this—they lose their importance with the passing of time. Not only that, but it would be quite an expensive proposition for someone to have that stone shipped back to the mainland and either have the surface smoothed down or else substitute a new stone entirely.

Weeks passed into months, months passed into years and eventually—well, what's the use of bothering about it at this late date?

Ocracoke enjoys the distinction of having had a citizen who died thirteen years before being born, according to pretty good evidence.

Ducks and Geese

I've already admitted that I'm a sorry fisherman. The same thing applies to duck and goose hunting.

I've never shot a duck or goose in all my life. Come to think of it, I've never shot anything except maybe a sparrow or two with a Daisy air rifle.

You see, I spent the early years of my life up in New York state, just about 25 miles up from New York City, and we never had any shooting to amount to anything. Maybe a few squirrels, but that's about all. Here in North Carolina most boys are taken hunting by their dads or older brothers just as soon as they are able to tote a gun. They shoot quail, deer, turkeys, ducks, geese and a lot of other things. Hunting is as much a part of their lives as baseball, football or swimming.

There are a number of blinds scattered along the sound side of Ocracoke but there isn't as much hunting now as there was fifteen or twenty years ago. They still kill quite a number of ducks and geese, however.

I visited the island last January and asked Stanley Wahab, "How's the hunting this season?"

135

"Well, unless we have good weather for it, it's poor," he replied.

"What do you mean by good weather?"

"Bad weather."

"Come again?"

"What you call good weather—nice and warm with the sun shining brightly—is bad weather for hunting. When it's raw and cold outside, with the temperature 'way down, and perhaps a slight drizzle of rain falling, it's good weather. When you go out hunting in that kind of weather you usually don't have any trouble killing your limit. But in fair weather the ducks and geese don't move around very much. They'll stay just outside of shooting range, apparently perfectly happy and contented. You can sit in your blind all day long but they won't come any closer."

Stanley used to operate a hunting lodge near the northern end of the island, but all that territory has now been taken over by the National Parks Commission.

The federal government fixes the dates for hunting migratory fowl, and these dates may be changed from year to year. The season for shooting ducks usually runs from the middle of November to the early part of January. The bag limit is three ducks daily. The season for geese extends over this same period but you're allowed to bring in only two geese per day.

There are game wardens all along the coast who see to it that the regulations are obeyed.

Canada geese come to Ocracoke every year in fairly large numbers. Brant also offer mighty fine

shooting. Then there are the four primary species of diving ducks—redheads, canvasbacks, greater scaup and lesser scaup. The last two also are known as blue bills or blackheads.

In addition to the above there's the American coot, known locally as a blue peter. There also are tipping ducks—pintails and black ducks—and there are other varieties in lesser numbers.

If you live outside of North Carolina you've got

137

to get a hunting license before you can start shooting ducks or geese. Or anything else, for that matter. This license costs you $15.75 for the season. If you are a resident of the state you also have to buy a license, of course, but you get it cheaper. The cost of a hunting license is $3.10, or a combination license, for hunting and fishing, for $4.10.

There are people—people of good judgment, plenty of common sense, normal in every respect—who have been coming to Ocracoke for years to shoot ducks and geese. They get up at 5:30 in the morning, have themselves rowed out to a blind, sit in a drizzling rain for hours and hours, sometimes kill their limit, sometimes not getting a single shot, pay for the services of a guide, pay out a lot of money for traveling expenses, hotel bills and other items and claim that they're having the grandest time in the world.

To me it doesn't make sense, but I realize I'm not normal when it comes to hunting.

When it comes to eating migratory fowl, however, I'm right there with the rest of you people. There's nothing I like better than a wild duck—and a goose is a close second.

Take one of these wild fowl and bake it as it should be baked. (I believe there are various kinds of stuffing that can be used but I'm not an expert in the culinary art so I won't go into this.) Be sure to have plenty of wild rice and gravy. *Plenty of gravy!* Green peas make a nice addition also. Give yourself plenty of elbow room, take the duck in your fingers, and brother, you've got something there that's simply delicious.

One thing I've never been able to understand about ducks and geese. As the hunting season progresses they become cagier and cagier. They have found out the significance of a blind and shy away from it. But the day following the closing of the season, those same ducks and geese will light in the middle of Silver Lake or in close proximity to the blinds with never a sign of anxiety or fear.

Maybe they've got a built-in calendar, or something.

The Coast Guard

What Reynolds Tobacco Company means to Winston-Salem, Cannon Mills means to Kannapolis, Tomlinson means to High Point and the University of North Carolina means to Chapel Hill—the Coast Guard means to Ocracoke.

There are several reasons for this.

In the first place, there are about forty or fifty retired Coast Guardmen or their widows who live on the island. They receive regular monthly checks from the government and these checks play an important part in the economic picture of Ocracoke.

In the second place, there are 25 men in active service on the island; fourteen in the station proper and eleven aboard the 83-footer which makes its home base at the dock in front of the station. These men are also paid regularly and they spend practically every penny, except what they save, at home.

If the money paid to the active and retired Coast Guardmen was taken from Ocracoke, the island would be in the same fix as Pitt County without a tobacco crop, Gaston County without its cotton mills and Moore County without its peaches.

The station is a three-story frame structure, painted white and always kept in the best of condition. Boat houses and repair shops are also immaculate. The installation is located on the north side of the narrow inlet which connects Silver Lake with Pamlico Sound, a most strategic spot from several points of view.

Youngsters in different parts of the country have different ambitions. Some want to be aviators, others want to be policemen, still others want to emulate Davey Crockett. On Ocracoke the prevailing ambition among boys is to become members of the Coast Guard.

You know how it is in your home town; how people look upon the leading merchant, the banker, the outstanding lawyer, the preacher and so on. Well, a Coast Guardman on the outer banks is held in similar regard and esteem.

In order to bring you some authentic information

about the operation of the station, I spent an after-noon there sometime ago talking to the chief and several of the men, all of whom had been in the service for many years.

Would you like to join? The first thing a new man does is to file an application in the district office located in Norfolk. In due course, if his application is acted upon favorably, he is called to Norfolk and is given a physical examination. If he passes that, he is sent to boot camp at Cape May, New Jersey.

His course of training there takes a period of 13 weeks. When he has completed it, he is sent to a district that has put in an application for new men. The officer in charge of the district sends him to a station which requires personnel replacement.

The starting pay is $85 a month, which includes room and board and an allowance for clothing.

The new man starts out as a recruit. Then, if he makes good, he becomes a seaman first class. From there he advances to third-class petty officer, second-class petty officer, first-class petty officer and finally, if he can qualify, chief. Each advancement in rank carries with it an increase in pay.

The commanding officer of a station is not referred to as Captain; he's Chief.

One of the men at the station told me that the average retirement pay is $175.00 a month. This surprised me somewhat because I had thought it was much lower than that. Possibly $100.00 or $125.00.

Down on Ocracoke Island, $175.00 a month ain't hay.

Here's the daily routine of activity at the station:

The men get up at 6:30 and clean up their quarters. Breakfast is served at 7 o'clock. From 7:30 to 8 the men spend their time cleaning or painting equipment and making sure that everything is in neat order on the property.

Colors at 8 o'clock. Then a continuation of work. Chow is served at noon. The men carry on such duties as may be assigned them by the Chief. They knock off work at 4:30 and from then on they're on their own until the following morning.

All but one of them, that is. A lookout is kept in the tower constantly. The men take turns at maintaining four-hour watches.

What kind of work is the Coast Guard called upon to perform?

Most people, when this branch of the service is mentioned, immediately think of shipwrecks. That used to be true in the old days of sailing ships, when navigation was a rather sketchy science and when there were no means of communication with shore stations or other vessels. In the modern era of radio and radar, however, wrecks on the ocean side of the island are infrequent. About the only way a wreck could happen would be for the captain and the crew to be down below decks, playing gin rummy.

Most of the activity of the Coast Guard today is concentrated in the sound. Shrimpers get nets tangled up in the screws of their boats: the Coast Guard is called upon for help. A yacht gets aground in Pamlico Sound or some other place along the Inland Waterway;

again it's up to the Coast Guard to render assistance. The 83-footer is used for most of this work. When help is needed out in the ocean, one of the lifeboats is taken out. These boats can weather any kind of a storm. A huge wave may capsize them but when the wave has gone on its way, the boat rights itself. The maneuver is almost like a slow roll in an airplane.

One of the lifeboats is 38 feet long; the other is two feet shorter.

Speaking of airplanes, there are quite a number of these landing on Ocracoke and elsewhere along the outer banks. Sometimes the planes run into soft sand while taxiing and nose over. It's up to the Coast Guard to straighten things out.

In any kind of emergency, the first thing that people on the island think of is the Coast Guard—fire, sudden illness, hurricane damage, ships in distress and so on.

A number of years ago there were 25 Coast Guard stations along the North Carolina coast. There has been a lot of consolidation work going on during the last ten or fifteen years and now there are only eleven in North Carolina territory. The reason: a much larger area of beach can be patrolled today than was the case in the past. Modern equipment has made this possible. And so, after all is said and done, the eleven stations are rendering just as good service today, if not better, than the twenty-five stations did a score of years ago.

No Juvenile Delinquency

Many people today are claiming that the younger generation is going to the dogs.

That may be true about boys and girls in some localities but it certainly isn't true of the youngsters on Ocracoke.

Instead of going to the dogs, the younger generation goes fishing, pony riding, sailing or swimming.

They haven't much time for delinquency: there are too many other things to occupy their minds.

At one time Ocracoke had the only mounted Boy Scout troop in the country, and you ought to have seen how those boys could ride! No saddle or bridle: they were considered superfluous. However, there aren't as many ponies on the island as there used to be, so the boys now do most of their scouting afoot or in boats.

Most of the credit in connection with formation of the Boy Scout troop must be given Colonel Marvin W. Howard, native Ocracoker who has led an adventuresome life for many years. He's a veteran of both World Wars and was the first army officer to sail as commander of a fleet of merchant vessels, including several large dredges, across the Atlantic to England and France to assist in removing navigational hazards. He continued dredge work after the war in Mexico, California and Venezuela.

A couple of years ago he said he was through: that all he wanted from then on was to live on Ocracoke Island.

He organized the Boy Scouts in 1954 and taught the boys how to tame the wild ponies and also how to ride. He, himself, is a great horseman, the son of another great rider, Homer Howard. Along with his Boy Scout work, Marvin also is doing all he can to persuade the Park Service to try and make some arrangements whereby the ponies may be kept on the island.

Getting back to juvenile delinquency again: what is said to be responsible for breeding this condition among our young people today?

Extreme poverty, for one thing. Broken homes. Idleness. Indifference on the part of parents. Trying to ape gangsters and other tough characters. Organized gangs of hoodlums.

There's none of that on Ocracoke. In many respects, the population is just one big family. There's a lot of relationship among the islanders. If little Jimmy starts cutting up and developing traits that are not approved of, chances are that Uncle Luke, Aunt Martha, Cousin Louise or Grandpappy Garrish will spot him and make a report to his parents.

That's a mighty discouraging situation if you're

trying to make progress as a juvenile delinquent.

In most towns of any size there are disreputable joints which may attract some of the boys in the community—places where they develop a liking for gambling, for stealing, for associating with all kinds of bad company and staying up until all hours of the night. You don't find these temptations on Ocracoke. The rule of early to bed and early to rise is followed pretty closely on the island by young and old alike. And, as I've mentioned before, there are so many means of healthful, clean recreation that the youngsters don't have much time for anything else.

One final thing: there are no stores on the island that display sensational comic books or obscene magazines of the type that you find in drugstores, newsstands and other establishments on the mainland.

All in all, the young folks on the island are clean-cut youngsters—boys and girls alike—and it's very seldom indeed that they cause their parents any worry because of bad conduct on their part.

The Wreck of the Ariosto

There have been hundreds of shipwrecks along the North Carolina coast. The Diamond Shoals area, off Cape Hatteras, just north of Ocracoke, has been the cause of more wrecks than any other spot along the coast.

Since official records were started it is known that there have been forty wrecks off Ocracoke. This does not include boats of less than 50 tons.

Mention already has been made of the *Carroll A. Deering*, the "ghost ship" that refused to stay put. Another wreck that the islanders still talk about occured in December, 1899, and involved the *Ariosto*, a tramp steamer with schooner-rigged sails, bound from Galveston to Hamburg, via Norfolk.

Captain R. R. Baines was in command. The ship ran into stormy weather as she proceeded up the coast. The evening of December 23 had been clear but toward midnight rain squalls were passing over the vessel. The wind also increased appreciably.

At 3:45 a.m., Christmas Eve, Captain Baines was summoned on deck and one of the mates called his attention to the "white water" which surrounded the *Ariosto*, indicating that she was in extremely shallow water. Before the course could be changed, the ship struck bottom, hesitated a moment and then careened badly over on her starboard side.

The entire crew of thirty were summoned on deck and the rocket signals of distress were fired. Following a brief interval, a red flash was seen from the north, which the Captain assumed as meaning that assistance might come from that source. He was correct in that but he was 'way off in another respect.

His impression was that the *Ariosto* had grounded on Diamond Shoals. The answering rocket flash had come from the north. There is no land north of Diamond Shoals.

Captain Baines was under great tension and failed to take this fact into consideration. The vessel was pounding on the sandbar. He feared that in a very short while she would break in two and that everyone aboard would be drowned.

He gave the order to abandon ship.

It was a disastrous decision. The *Ariosto* was not grounded on Diamond Shoals but had struck some 15 miles to the southwest and close to the beach of Ocracoke Island. Land could not be discerned because of the darkness and rain squalls.

Help from the Life Saving station (the Coast Guard service was known by that name in those days) was on the way. If the men had remained aboard ship everyone undoubtedly would have been saved.

Two of the *Ariosto's* boats were lowered away and

the men crowded into them. Both were cast loose from the ship before all the members of the crew could reach them. This meant that four men, including Captain Baines, were left on the ship.

The two boats—a mate in command of each—stood by the *Ariosto* waiting the coming of dawn. In the course of half an hour or so, the two boats capsized and of the twenty-six men aboard, only two managed to swim back to the *Ariosto*. The others were left to struggle in the sea.

When members of the Ocracoke Life Saving station arrived on the beach opposite the stranded vessel, they discovered a lone figure staggering toward them. The lifesavers had had trouble getting their equipment up the beach and this had delayed them considerably. It was approximately an hour and a half after the *Ariosto's* first distress signal that the lifesavers appeared on the scene.

The man approaching them was Seaman Karl Elsing who had managed to swim ashore. He gave them a hurried account of what had taken place.

The lifesavers set up their equipment in the darkness and an experimental shot was fired in the direction of the steamer. It fell short and all hands immediately began to haul in the line.

Then a miracle happened. The line pulled heavily. The men continued to haul. At the end was Boatswain Aleck Anderson, the line wrapped around one of his arms. He had been swimming desperately in the effort to keep his head above water. Not being an expert, he was about to give up when the line, fired in the direction of the steamer, hit him across the shoulder. He had strength enough to seize it and wrap it about his arm securely. When he landed on the beach he was in a half-drowned condition but he revived rapidly and was able to assist in the rescue work.

By this time it was beginning to get light. Another member of the crew (his name has been forgotten) managed to swim ashore. More shots were fired toward the steamer and one of these landed on the forward part of the craft where one of the men grabbed hold of it and made it fast. The rest of the line was then hauled aboard and the heavy hawser attached to the other end was also pulled in and made fast.

But the ship was lying broadside to the beach and, with every sea, she rolled first toward and then away from the land, dipping the hawser first into the water, then snapping it out. There was constant danger that it might be severed. At 2:30 p.m. the last man aboard, Captain Baines, reached the beach, and the large crowd that had assembled by that time gave a loud cheer.

Twenty-one men lost their lives. They perished because of the dreadful name of Diamond Shoals, which had caused their captain to make a serious mistake in judgment. Had he analyzed the situation carefully, he would have known better than to let the two lifeboats cast off from the ship.

IN MEMORY OF
ANN HOWARD.
WIFE OF GEORGE HOWARD
BORN ———— 1724
DIED NOVEMBER 24ᵗʰ 1841
AGED 117 YEARS

LO! the prisoner is released,
Lightened of her fleshly load.
Where the weary are at rest,
She is gathered unto God.

The Oldest Resident

Ann Howard must have been the oldest person ever to have lived in North Carolina.

Her grave is located in the Howard family cemetery. She was the wife of the first Howard settler on the island. The inscription on her tombstone says that she was born in 1724 and died in 1841, which would make her 117 years old.

Ocracokers Stay Put

As a general thing—once an Ocracoker, always an Ocracoker.

At least that's the impression one would get as a result of checking the population today with what it was when the first national census was taken in 1790.

That particular census lists these names among the residents of the island more than 160 years ago—Williams, Gaskins, Garrish, O'Neal, Jackson, Daniels, Salter and Scarborough.

Those same names are prominent on the island today.

Of course there has been emigration and also some immigration down throughout the years, but most of the present residents can trace their ancestry back four or five generations. All of them have been Ocracokers.

Where did the early settlers come from?

Well, there are several intriguing stories told about this. Some people hold that the first-comers were shipwrecked sailors who decided to remain on the island after having been washed ashore. I've even heard it said that many of today's residents are descendants of pirates. All of which makes interesting conversation and reading but it isn't true.

For the most part, the early settlers of Ocracoke ambled down this way from points in Virginia. They liked what they found on the outer banks and made up their minds to stay there.

Their descendants, apparently arrived at the same decision.

News Travels Fast

One of the finest "grapevines" you've ever seen exists on the island. Ocracokers now have telephone service but they don't need it in helping spread the news. As soon as something happens, practically everybody knows about it in a matter of minutes. I recall this little incident which happened during one of my visits down there.

C. F. Boyette operated the local picture theatre. On this particular day he failed to receive the film for the regular Saturday night performance. It was supposed to have come at 4:30 on the mail boat but had missed connections somewhere along the line.

The show was supposed to start at seven o'clock.

Mr. Boyette double checked with Mrs. Howard, postmaster. The latter told him that the film wasn't in the mail; that it couldn't possibly have been overlooked.

That's all that was said.

Did a lot of people show up for the evening performance and were they disappointed to learn that there would be no show?

Not by a long shot. Nobody was disappointed because everybody had heard that the film had failed to arrive.

It's the same way with practically everything else. If Elmo Fulcher's shrimp boat comes back into port with an extraordinary catch of shrimp, the news is all over the island almost before Elmo can get his boat tied up at the dock.

If Congressman Herbert Bonner should arrive by boat and land at the Coast Guard dock, his presence would be known generally before he had shaken a dozen hands.

And as for somebody dying or a new baby appearing on the scene, it's old news in no time at all.

She Never Had Been Off the Island

During the course of my many visits to the outer banks I tried for a number of years to find a person who never had been to the mainland. I asked about this at Portsmouth, Ocracoke, Hatteras, Rodanthe, Avon and other communities but it looked as though my quest would be in vain.

I met a few individuals who had been on the mainland only four or five times since they were born but that's as far as I was able to go.

Looked as though everybody had been off the banks at least once in his lifetime.

One day, while compiling material for this book, I was eating lunch at the Ocracoke Coffee Shoppe, as it was known in those days. It is now known as the Island Inn.

Liz Styron used to do most of the cooking at the inn. She is known to many visitors because she used to cook at Captain Bill Gaskill's place about forty years ago. And when it comes to preparing clam chowder, clam fritters and other seafood dishes, Liz is in a class by herself.

While I was getting away with a bowl of chowder I asked Liz how long it had been since she had visited the mainland.

"About seven months."

"I imagine that some of the people don't leave the island as much as once a year, do they?"

"Some never leave at all."

"Never leave? I certainly would like to meet someone who never has been off the island. You don't happen to know of one, do you?"

"I sure do."

"Who is it?

"My sister, Eliza Ella. She's Mrs. Ivey O'Neal and she never has been off Ocracoke except maybe a mile or so while fishing in a small boat. I know that's the truth because she has told me so many times."

"How come she never has been to the mainland?"

"I don't know: I reckon she just hasn't wanted to go. But why don't you go and ask her? She lives across the creek near where the old hotel used to be."

When I had finished my lunch I went out to call on Mrs. O'Neal. I found the house without difficulty near the southern end of the village. She lived at that time with her son and daughter-in-law, Mr. and Mrs. John O'Neal, and was doing some work among the flowers in her yard as I approached.

After I had introduced myself, I told her what Liz had said and then I asked how come she never had had any desire to travel.

"Well," she said, "it's like this. When I was a child nobody ever offered to take me, and when I got a little older I never particularly wanted to go."

Her daughter-in-law chimed in: "My people live in Windsor, Bertie County, and I've tried to get Mamma to go with me on a visit to them but I gave it up several years ago. I can't get her to do it to save my life."

"But haven't you ever had any desire to see what the outside world looks like?" I inquired. "Don't you think you'd be interested in seeing the sights in a big city, or the mountains in western North Carolina, or the fine stores and other attractions?"

"Different people have different ideas," was her response. "I'm interested in my relatives and friends here on the island. I'm interested when a new baby is born or when someone makes a big catch of fish. I like to watch the boats on Silver Lake, and I like to wake up in the morning to the sound of ducks quacking and geese honking. Everyone has his own likes and dislikes. Some people like to travel while others like to stay at home. I'm one of those that likes to stay at home."

"Seems to me you'd feel as though you've missed a lot," I protested.

"You don't miss the things you don't know about. If you've always lived in a little house like ours, you don't miss a big mansion. Ocracoke is the finest place in the world to me because I don't know anything about other places. The people are the finest in the world because I don't know any others. The folks who live in big cities are always conscious of the fact that some of their neighbors live in better houses than they do, or are richer than they are. This brings about a lot of discontent, jealousy and unhappiness. But we don't have anything like that on the island. With very few exceptions all of us are practically on the same level. We enjoy the same things and we live more or less in the same manner. There's none of this foolishness about keeping up with the Joneses because there are no Joneses here to keep up with. We don't have any crime—no robberies, no murders or anything like that. People go to church on Sundays and teach their children to go to Sunday school. When anyone gets sick, the neighbors help take care of them. All this may seem to be rather a tame way of living, so far as some of the people on the mainland are concerned, but we enjoy it here and I'm perfectly happy and contented."

This interview took place a number of years ago. Mrs. O'Neal at that time was about 63 years old. Just as friendly, vivacious a person as you'd want to meet. She interested herself in the affairs of her neighbors, was always ready to be of service to those in any kind of difficulty or trouble and was held in high regard by everyone on the island.

It so happened that I had flown down in my own plane. Before leaving Mrs. O'Neal I told her about this. "How about flying back to Raleigh with me and spending the week-end?" I suggested. "Mrs. Goerch will be only too glad to have you visit at our home and I'd like to put you on my radio program Sunday night."

163

She smiled brightly. "No thank you, although I appreciate the offer very much. I was born on Ocracoke, I've lived here ever since I was born and I expect to die here."

Her expectations were fulfilled because she passed away about two years later after a lingering illness. She died without ever having left the island.

Some Other Shipwrecks

Mention already has been made of two outstanding shipwrecks off Ocracoke—the *Carroll A. Deering* and the *Ariosto*—but so far as loss of life is concerned, the worst wreck in Ocracoke waters was that of the steam packet, *Home*, in 1837.

Ninety people were drowned as the result of this maritime mishap.

The *Home* was a paddle-wheel steamer. She also had sails. Her overall length was 210 feet and she was regarded as being the fastest packet engaged in coast-wise service between New York and Charleston.

A new ship, built the year before, she was popular as a result of the enviable record she had made in speedy transportation. Only two trips had been made between New York and Charleston before she was wrecked.

The *Home* ran into stormy weather soon after she left New York harbor. Off Cape Hatteras the winds had reached hurricane force. The craft shipped vast quantities of water which the pumps were unable to handle. Passengers were called upon to help bail out the ship, but their desperate efforts proved futile.

The velocity of the wind increased. It appeared as though the *Home* would capsize at any moment. The water continued to rise and soon reached the engine fires. The engines stopped and the vessel was completely at the mercy of the sea.

She rolled onward. Suddenly there was a trembling motion followed by a sudden jolt. The *Home* had struck the beach about four miles northeast of the village of Ocracoke.

It was 10 o'clock at night. Rain was falling in torrents, whipped viciously by the high winds. Visibility was practically nil. The packet was approximately one hundred yards from land.

Panic ensued. The screams of women and children could be heard above the fury of the storm. Male passengers and members of the crew worked frantically in an endeavor to launch lifeboats. There were three aboard. The first was crushed as it smashed up against the side of the vessel. The same fate befell the second. The third had seventeen passengers aboard. It swung clear of the *Home* but in a moment it capsized and everyone was thrown into the foaming waters.

Women and children were directed to go to the bow, which was closer to the shore than any other part of the ship. They stood there, continuing to cry out in terror.

There were only two life-preservers aboard the Home.

Those were the days before vessels were made to carry one life-preserver for every person aboard.

Passengers and crew numbered 130.

The tremendous waves continued to beat against

the *Home*. The forecastle broke away from the rest of the ship, carrying women and children into the waters. Practically all perished.

The vessel continued to disintegrate. Passengers picked up anything that would float—chairs, spars, oars, doors torn from hinges, etc.,—and used these items in an endeavor to reach shore.

Some succeeded: others died in the attempt.

People of the island were standing on the beach but were unable to give aid other than forming a human life-line and dragging survivors ashore.

One hundred and thirty souls aboard.

Ninety of these perished.

Those who managed to reach shore were taken into homes of the islanders until they were in condition to leave. Some had been severely injured and were kept in bed for a week or more before they could be moved.

Ninety lives lost. The worst maritime tragedy in the history of Ocracoke.

Twenty-one were lost on the *Ariosto*.

All in all, there have been thirty-five vessels that grounded on Ocracoke and were completely demolished. This was during the period from 1814 to 1942. In addition, there were other craft that got into trouble but were saved.

But listen to this: in 1942 there were 81 vessels—most of them oil tankers—sunk off the coast of North Carolina. There were five in 1943 and one in 1945. (This was during World War II.)

Thirty or forty years ago, when I first started going to Ocracoke more or less regularly, you could see at least a score of wrecked hulls along the beach between the village and Hatteras Inlet. The sand has covered most of these. Others have been torn loose by the wind and high tides and have washed out to sea. You'll still see signs of a few wrecks but not nearly as many as was the case in years gone by.

And, so far as that goes, there are nowhere nearly as many shipwrecks off the island today as there were fifty or a hundred years ago. What with radio, radar and other modern means of communication, it is almost impossible to conceive how a wreck could take place.

But—you never can tell. Look what happened to that Italian luxury liner and the Swedish ship not so long ago. Despite all of our modern precautions against disaster of that nature, they ran into each other and a number of lives were lost.

Another thing that should be brought out in connection with these shipwrecks off Ocracoke; the people of the island—Coast Guardsmen and civilians alike—never waver in their efforts to be of every possible assistance when a vessel is in distress. They'll risk their lives, they'll go without sleep for many hours, they'll gladly take the survivors into their homes, and they'll do everything else they can to help those who need help.

As Big Ike remarked to me one day: "We know what those people are up against because we've had many close calls ourselves. Anybody who lives as close to the sea as we do is always ready to answer any call that comes from the sea."

Use of Motor Vehicles

Owning and operating an automobile or truck on Ocracoke is slightly different from what it is on the mainland.

In the first place, cars wear out much faster on the island. The salt air and sand are anything but beneficial. Then too, most cars remain out in the open all the time instead of being put up in garages. On top of all this, traffic conditions are rather strenuous. Many times, when a man wants to drive his car over to the beach, he has to drive through water a foot deep for half a mile or more.

That isn't good for a car. Nor is continuous driving in low or second gear over some of the heavy, sandy routes.

When a man on the mainland has driven his automobile or truck for two, three, five or ten years he usually trades it in on a new car. The dealer takes the old car off his hands.

On Ocracoke there are no automobile dealers. A man drives his car until she's ready to give up the ghost. In most instances he is able to do his own repair work, for your average Ocracoker is a good carpenter, house-painter, plumber and auto mechanic. He'll keep that car of his running as long as it is humanly possible to do so. The original paint job begins to fade at the end of a year or so. After that, the appearance of the car becomes steadily worse. Signs

of rust and corrosion multiply. The engine develops a knock that seems to be characteristic of cars on Ocracoke after they've been driven any length of time. Finally, when she gives her last gasp, the owner leaves her where she is—by the side of the road or out on the beach—after removing tires and a few other things which he might want to use for spare parts on his next car.

The trade-in value of such a pile of junk is practically nil.

As you wander over the island you'll come across several of these discarded automobiles. They don't add particularly to the beauty of the landscape but what is a man to do with them?

Until recently, the automobile owners of Ocracoke didn't have to buy any state license plates because there were no state-controlled roads on the island. Now, however, with the coming of a new state highway from the northern tip of the island to the village, everybody has to purchase a state tag.

Drivers of autos and trucks seem to take a strange delight in going 'round and 'round on the four or five miles of narrow pavement in the village. Last time I was at Ocracoke, taking a walk after supper, I met the same car half a dozen times before I got back to the hotel.

Nobody drives faster than twenty miles an hour because of the narrow pavement and the many sharp turns. The hot-rod boys take their cars out on the sand flat just east of the village and there they can zoom along at sixty miles an hour if they so desire. The hard, smooth sand makes an excellent race track. However, as a rule, there is very little speeding done.

The most popular car is the jeep. With four-wheel drive there's no danger of an experienced driver getting stuck anywhere on the island.

Soda Pop Is in Demand

Of course I don't know where I could get accurate statistics on this subject, but I'd be willing to bet that there is more soda pop drunk by children on the island—in proportion to population—than is the case anywhere else in the United States.

Give a child on the mainland a quarter and there's no telling what he'll do with it. Give an Ocracoke boy or girl a quarter and the first thing they'll do will be to run to the nearest store and purchase a bottle of pop.

The bigger the bottle, the more popular the drink. Fruit drinks—orange, grape, etc.—are especially in demand.

While on the island recently, I walked from the Wahab Village Hotel to the Community Store—about a quarter of a mile or so. Just for the fun of it, I kept count. I met seventeen children—some on bicycles—and of this number, eleven had soda-pop bottles in their hands.

Big Jake and Little Jake

While you're at Ocracoke you want to be sure to visit Channel Bass Inn.

When the sign was first put up over the front door of the place it read like this: "Chanel Bass Inn."

It's the only spot on the island that approaches what might be called a night club and it's operated by Jake Alligood, his wife and their son. Father and son are distinguished by calling one Big Jake and the other Little Jake.

Big Jake will talk your head off if you give him half a chance but you have to work mighty hard to get a few words out of Little Jake.

Ask Big Jake about the weather and he'll not only tell you what's likely to happen in the immediate future but he'll also expatiate on what has happened during the last week or so.

Ask Little Jake, "Do you think we'll have good weather tomorrow?" and he'll go into deep thought. He'll consider the matter from every point of view, realizing the seriousness of such a query. Then, after thorough deliberation, he'll tell you, "Maybe."

The inn is a quonset hut, located a hundred yards or so from the Wahab Village Hotel. It has been enlarged during the last couple of years and is now twice its original size.

Jake lives in a comfortable house a few yards from the inn. He keeps ducks. At five o'clock in the morning

175

177

these ducks stage a parade which takes them toward the hotel. They don't have a band, so they march to the tune of loud quacking. This wakes up most of the guests whose rooms are on that side of the hotel. In many instances these guests lean out of their windows and cuss the ducks with considerable fluency and thoroughness, thinking to scare them away, but it doesn't work. The ducks probably think they're being encouraged, so they quack all the louder.

All this noise wakes up other guests in the building who thereupon vent their spleen on the ones doing the shouting at the ducks.

It's all sort of disheartening to the guy who has come to Ocracoke in the hope of being able to sleep as late as he wants to.

Inside Jake's place you'll find a small store at which you can purchase canned goods, all kinds of soda pop, ice cream, cigarettes and so on. There's a small dance floor, about 24 feet square. Benches line the walls, and over near one of the windows is a juke box.

'Long about 6:30, after they've finished eating supper, the young folks begin to arrive. They drink pop and play the juke box. Occasionally they'll start a square dance. Visitors join in the dancing.

The place closes promptly at ten o'clock. If you're over at the hotel you can hear the blaring of the juke box very plainly, but inasmuch as quitting time is early, you don't mind this particularly. You can go to bed after ten o'clock and sleep in perfect peace until those darned ducks start quacking in the morning.

Jake, up to the present time, has never won a beauty

contest, and there are folks who will bet you ten to one that he never will. His face is seamy and weather-beaten, brown as an Indian. He has lost a few of his teeth. There's one thing, however, about which he is very particular: he shaves once a week and insists upon Little Jake doing the same thing.

In addition to running Channel Bass Inn, Jake and Little Jake also are in the taxicab business. They've got two four-wheel-drive trucks which they use in meeting the mail boat and in carrying fishermen up and down the length of the island. The fishermen are put off at some suitable location and Jake tells them when he'll be back for them.

The village, as I've mentioned before, is located a mile from the ocean and it is necessary to cross the broad sand flat in order to get to the beach. Most folks

179

don't like to walk this distance, particularly when the sand is hot, so they get Jake to taxi them across.

The charge for this service? There's no fixed price. Usually Jake leaves it up to his passengers to fix the rate and, as a rule, they're inclined to be rather liberal.

During the hunting season Jake stays pretty busy also. Operation of the inn and the taxicab company combine in assuring him and his family a comfortable living.

I'm sorry to report that during the last year or so, Big Jake's eyes have been going bad on him. Last spring his condition became worse and as this is being written he is totally blind. There's some talk of an operation but I don't know whether this will take place or not.

Garbage Disposal

Until recently there was no garbage disposal plant on the island.

What did they do with garbage and other rubbish?

Well, some of it they buried in their own back yard, particularly when they cleaned fish. It made fine fertilizer. But most of it was carried by truck out on the sand flat where it was dumped and allowed to remain.

This was done for two reasons. The first, of course, was that it helped get rid of the garbage. The second was that it helped start sand dunes and tended to build up the beach. Here's how it worked:

A pile of rubbish was thrown out on the beach. The sand would blow up against it. Day by day the little pile was covered with more and more sand. In due course, the rubbish disappeared completely, and you'd only see the sand. With the passing of the years, the pile kept on growing and growing and eventually it became a full-sized sand dune.

But no longer is rubbish permitted to be dumped in the sand. Ocracoke now has a community dump in which the people get rid of their garbage.

School and the Rondthalers

Having read this far, you should be convinced by now that Ocracoke is different in many respects from communities on the mainland.

This difference also applies to educational facilities for its boys and girls.

Before going into that, however, let me first tell you something about the Rondthalers—Theodore and Alice.

In Nebraska, Maine or Wisconsin, that name—Rondthaler—may not have any special significance, but here in North Carolina it is outstanding. For many years it has been associated with the Moravian Church. Theodore's father, Dr. Howard E. Rondthaler, was president of Salem College in Winston-Salem. Theodore's grandfather, Edward Rondthaler, was bishop of the Moravian Church from 1891 to 1931. There is no more highly respected name in this state than that of Rondthaler.

Almost 30 years ago, Mr. and Mrs. Theodore Rondthaler moved to Ocracoke. They moved there because, as a result of one or two previous visits, they had learned to like the island and its people. They took charge of the school. They interested themselves in civic and community affairs. Today they are considered as much a part of Ocracoke as the lighthouse or the Coast Guard station, and are accepted as such by the people generally.

When outsiders come to live in a community their motives and intentions are often criticised. I can honestly say, however, that I have never heard a word of criticism concerning the Rondthalers. There's a mutual liking and understanding existing between them and the natives of the island.

When the wind blows right you can hear the surf through the windows of the Ocracoke school building. It's a modest, one-story frame structure, divided into six rooms, including the library. When the Rondthalers were there, there were three other teachers, ninety pupils and twelve grades.

Isolation could be a handicap to a school, but such is not the case here. An extremely active and loyal P.T.A. works constantly and enthusiastically at ways and means of improving educational facilities. Money is raised by suppers and local-talent shows, and the proceeds go for purchasing library books, instructional and recreational supplies, records, pictures, charts, encyclopedias, maps, drawing materials, laboratory supplies and athletic equipment of all kinds. In addition to all this, the P.T.A. will undertake without hesitation such ambitious proposals as buying venetian blinds for those rooms that happen to be exposed to too much sunshine, equipment for a kitchenette, stage fittings, ping-pong tables and numerous other items. All in all, the local P.T.A. has earned and spent something like $800 a year, year after year, for the betterment of the Ocracoke school.

Let's see you find another community of 500 people with a record such as this.

Besides these physical values and the self-reliance required to achieve them, Ocracoke's isolation produces an interesting psychological value among its pupils; one that educators all over the country have pleaded for without much success. This is—sport for sport's sake, minus the bitter competitive element. Due to the fact that it is impossible to contact other schools, all sports on the island must be within the organization. As a consequence of this, sides must be on a "choose-up" basis. Who wins becomes much less important than just playing the game. This same spirit also allows much more widespread participation in games than in those schools where "the team's the thing." The less competent youngsters play happily alongside those who may be more proficient or skilled.

In a sense, Ocracoke school could be called five old-fashioned one-room schools in one building. Grades must be and are grouped, several under each teacher. The younger children learn from those that are older, and the older ones review their work by helping those of junior age. The high school course of study is rather traditional, consisting of the standard four years of English, two of algebra, one of geometry, three of social sciences, two of pure science, two of Latin, two of typewriting and commercial work, and two of health and physical education. This, plus the regular elementary offering, keeps all concerned well occupied.

The safety and parking of school busses is no problem: there are no school busses. The farthest-away pupil lives within a 15-minute walk of the building. The principal makes it from his house on a bicycle in five minutes. There is no cafeteria problem because all but half a dozen children walk home to lunch.

There's no problem of congestion in the corridors because there are no corridors. Each room has its own entrance to the outside.

On the playground the principal problem is playing games on the sandy soil. The ball won't bounce.

All in all, the school is doing its work in a highly efficient and effective manner. Credit for this is shared by the P.T.A., the principal and the teachers, and you might also include the entire population, because Ocracokers are keenly interested in providing proper educational facilities for their children.

The school is rated as being one of the best in all of Hyde County.

The Rondthalers retired as regular teachers several years ago, but Mrs. Rondthaler is sometimes called upon to help out in an emergency. Mr. Rondthaler passed away in the spring of 1966.

Bloodthirsty Teache

Reference to Edward Teache has been made in an earlier chapter which has to do with the naming of Ocracoke. It would hardly be treating the old boy fairly, however, if we didn't go just a bit more into detail about his career as one of the outstanding pirates ever to have plied his profession in North American waters.

Lafitte, Gasparillo, Bonney and others were all right in their way but they couldn't begin to compare with old Blackbeard.

He deserved his nickname. One of the proudest things he was of (there's sentence construction for you) was his beard. It grew all over his face—clear up to his eyes—and gave him a most ferocious appearance. He twisted the ends into pigtails, festooned with small ribbons. It is said that he spent considerable time daily, trimming or otherwise caring for it.

With a face like that, it would seem that all he had to do was to show himself while trying to capture a vessel and everyone would jump overboard.

The correct spelling of his name is uncertain. Some

writers have it Teach, others have it Teache. We'll string along with the latter.

Edward was born in Bristol, England, and went to sea at an early age. He got into the pirate business under the tutelage of Benjamin Thornigold, who merited the degree of Phi Beta Kappa in connection with the practice of his profession. Thornigold was a thorn in the flesh so far as shipping was concerned. He raided vessels on both sides of the Atlantic and belonging to all nationalities.

Young Teache was fascinated. He showed so much interest and demonstrated so much enthusiasm and energy that he soon became Thornigold's chief lieutenant.

On one occasion a French brig was captured. Teache asked Thornigold to let him take charge of the vessel. Some sort of agreement was made, after which Thornigold consented to let Teache go out on his own.

He was still in his early twenties. He named the brig *Queen Anne's Revenge*. She had forty guns aboard and it wasn't long after he had assumed command of the craft that her first capture was made.

Teache was in his element. He enjoyed the fighting and appreciated the plunder. It wasn't long before he was recognized as chief of the pirates, ranking even ahead of Thornigold.

On one occasion he sailed close to Charleston, anchoring *Queen Anne's Revenge* at the bar. He waited for a ship to come out. It wasn't long before one appeared, bound for London. Teache took her in charge. The same thing was done with three smaller craft.

Some of the folks aboard were permitted to go ashore but there were several prominent citizens of Charleston whom Teache kept as hostages. He sent two of his lieutenants to the city to get a chest of medicine. They brazenly walked through the streets of Charleston, making no effort to hide their identity. They told the Governor of Teache's request. They also told him of the prisoners Teache was holding. The upshot was that the Governor came across with the chest of medicinal supplies with the understanding that Teache would turn loose his prisoners.

Teache was as good as his word. He turned them loose, but before doing so, he picked them clean.

Up and down the Atlantic coast he carried on his maraudings. Shipping masters begged the authorities to do something about it. Eden was Governor of North Carolina at the time, making his residence in Bath Town. It was reported that he was in cahoots with Blackbeard. Anyway, he made no attempt to have the pirate apprehended.

Along with a lot of treasure he acquired as a result of his raids on shipping, Teache also acquired 13 wives. He fell in love with a girl of 15 and proceeded to marry her, too. Governor Eden performed the ceremony.

Finally Governor Spotswood of Virginia decided to see if Teache's operations couldn't be broken up. He offered liberal rewards for the capture of the ship and for the apprehending of Teache and his men.

There was a young naval officer up in Virginia by the name of Maynard. Lieutenant Robert Maynard.

189

He manned a couple of small ships and headed south, having received word that Teache and his men were in the vicinity of Ocracoke.

Blackbeard, in the meantime, also had learned that Maynard was on the way. He intended leaving his anchorage at Ocracoke and heading out into the sound, but it was too late to do this by daylight. The channels near the island were treacherous and curved in all directions. To a large extent they are in the same condition today. Anyway, Teache realized he would have to wait until morning before he could get away.

Morning came, and so did Maynard's two ships.

The fighting started and it must have been a lulu. Maynard concealed some of his men in the hold of one of his ships. Teache decided that most of the crew had been killed. He told his men to board Maynard's ship. They did, and when this took place, the men in the hold came up on deck and pitched into the pirates.

You've got to hand Blackbeard one thing: he was no coward. He received 20 saber cuts and 5 pistol wounds. He was about to cut Maynard in two with his sword when a sailor whanged him across the throat with the butt-end of his gun.

The story goes that Maynard stuck the pirate's head at the end of the vessel's bowsprit and sailed to Bath, where there was great rejoicing in which Governor Eden didn't participate. Then Maynard headed for the James River area, with the pirate's head still in the same position, and proceeded to collect the reward which he and his men had won.

Accommodations for Visitors

The question probably asked more than any other by people who never have visited the island is: "What kind of accomodations can one find there?"

The answer is—good.

Now don't get me wrong on that. If you're expecting anything like the high-falutin' hotels at Atlantic City, Virginia Beach, Miami and so on, you're going to be disappointed, because there's nothing like that at Ocracoke. You will find, however, clean rooms, comfortable beds and good food.

If that doesn't suit you, try some other place.

Old-timers still recall with a feeling of real nostalgia the old Pamlico Inn, run by Captain Bill Gaskill. Also the Gary Bragg House. And there were two or three other boarding establishments, and that was about all. But look at what has happened since then:

Today there are seven hotels and motels which afford first-class accommodations.

There are two tourist homes.

And there are twenty cottages with accommodations for two or more guests.

There are five cafes and restaurants.

There's a Park Information Center on the docks near the Coast Guard Station, and also a campground which is used by many vacationists.

And you can be sure of this: wherever you go, you'll get good food—particularly seafood of all kinds. By all means be sure to order clam chowder, because it is tastier at Ocracoke than any other place I've ever found.

Yes, Ocracoke has become modernized to a large degree but it still retains much of its old-time charm. And, as I've said before, if you want to visit a place that is "different," Ocracoke still fills the bill.

Until recently, practically every visitor to Ocracoke became acquainted with C. F. Boyette before leaving the island. For many years he was manager of the Wahab Village Hotel. And in later years he was desk man at the Pony Island Inn. Although not a native of the island (he was born in Johnston County) he was an enthusiastic booster. He died in 1967.

Religious Life

When I first began going to Ocracoke, about forty years ago, there were two Methodist churches—Northern Methodist and Southern Methodist. There was considerable rivalry between the two congregations, each striving to have a neater-looking building, each seeking to have the larger congregation.

This state of affairs continued until about twenty years ago when the two churches decided to unite and combine their efforts in making Ocracoke conscious of religion in a big way.

Now don't forget: there were two church buildings that had been in use for many years. Inasmuch as there was going to be only one congregation under the unification plan, you'd think that the members would decide on one or the other of the two buildings for their use. If neither structure was large enough, an addition could be added to it.

But this wasn't done. Southern Methodists said they didn't like the idea of worshiping in a Northern Methodist building: Northern Methodists held the same view with respect to holding meetings in the Southern building.

193

So what did they do? They tore down both edifices and built a new one out of the material that was salvaged.

But, as is often the case, there were a few individuals who didn't approve of all this. They refused to become a part of the united church. Some of them joined another church on the island—Assembly of God—and a few have quit going to church altogether.

The Assembly of God church is located in the southern part of the village; the Methodist church is adjacent to the schoolhouse.

I have talked to several old-timers about the single Methodist church on the island before the split took place. Many people have the idea that this split was brought about as a result of the War Between the States, but this isn't so. The separation took place a number of years later and was brought about because of a quarrel in connection with song books.

A singing teacher visited the island and wanted to teach the church members how to sing from books. One brother (a Howard) said this was all foolishness; that the singing was good enough when they h'isted the tune and he didn't see any reason for making a change and investing money in song books. But another brother (also a Howard) was equally vigorous in the contention that the singing would be greatly improved through the use of song books.

Each of the two Howards had his followers and the dissension became quite bitter. Some of the members dropped out and started a new church.

From what I've been able to find out, the new church was known as the Methodist South Church. The old one was known as the Methodist Episcopal Church. It had not been called the Northern Church because of any Yankee affiliation or sympathy but because it was north (in direction) from the other church.

The two Howard brothers whom I've mentioned were Coleman and Ellis Howard, but there seems to be some disagreement about which one did which.

And now, let's get back to the Methodist church of today.

I attended both Sunday school and morning services at the church recently. Sunday school got under way at ten o'clock. A few minutes before that time I arrived on the church grounds. About a score of adults and perhaps sixty or seventy children were standing outside, waiting for the bell to ring. When this occurred, the children went into their own room in the rear of the church; the grown-ups sat in different parts of the main auditorium.

The exterior of the church was painted white. So was the inside—both the walls and the pews—and trimmed in black. Chairs near the altar also were painted white with black cushions. Everything inside the building was as neat as a pin.

It was a hot, humid day. A few of the men wore coats but most of them were in sport shirts. I was glad to see this informality of attire; glad to see that the people were sensible about it instead of deliberately making themselves uncomfortable.

The superintendent of the Sunday school was Ben Spencer. He called on Brother Jonas Williams to lead in prayer. Brother Jonas is an elderly, heavy-set man. He knelt on one knee and rested his head on the back of the bench in front of him. He had a deep voice and his prayer was delivered in stentorian tones. It was an eloquent one without any fancy language. One couldn't help but be impressed with its heartfelt sincerity.

I talked with one of the members of the church after services and commented on the prayer. He nodded his head and said: "Yes, when Brother Jonas starts praying, the Lord stops whatever work He's doing and proceeds to listen."

We sang a hymn. Then the superintendent made one or two announcements, following which he said, "We will now take up the flower collection."

The plate was passed around and everyone put in

a coin. I asked about this when Sunday school came to a close and was told that a similar collection is taken up every first Sunday.

"Whenever anyone dies on the island," Ike O'Neal told me, "the Sunday school sends them flowers. It doesn't make any difference whether they are members of the church or Sunday school or not: we have been doing it for many years."

We sang a hymn and then the various classes assembled in groups and the lesson was taken up.

During the brief interlude between Sunday school and church services, many of the members introduced themselves to visitors in attendance and endeavored to let them know that they were welcome.

Rev. W. F. Hale was pastor. Shortly after the church services started and during the course of making some announcements, he told about his attendance at the District Methodist Conference.

"Needless to say," he stated, "I was deeply gratified to learn that our church, in proportion to its membership, has gained more new members during the last year than any church in the entire conference."

The congregation looked pleased.

Mr. Hale was a good preacher. He took as his text (if I can recall it correctly): "Fortunate is the land which has for its God the Lord." An excellent sermon which was received with close attention.

Many children remained for church services and I was impressed with their fine behavior.

Religion on the island is an orthodox proposition. New sects, new ideas and new theories may develop in other parts of the country and other parts of the world, but Ocracokers are fundamentalists in practically every respect. They accept their religion as it is set forth in the Bible, and it's very seldom that you hear any discussion or argument about whether this or that should be taken literally or not.

Remember the kind of religious faith that your grandfather and grandmother had?

That's the way the people of Ocracoke take their religion.

A Pirate Rendezvous

When piracy was in flower (If knighthood was in flower, why shouldn't piracy have been in flower also?) it was said that a number of freebooters used Ocracoke as a rendezvous. It was here that they repaired damage done to their vessels by storms or enemy attack. Naturally you'd presume that they buried part of their treasure here, too, but thus far nary a doubloon nor a piece of eight has been discovered. Not even so much as a piece of one.

Another thought might be that some of the pirates and their wives, or ladyfriends, remained on the island for various reasons, thereby becoming the ancestors of present-day residents. Maybe they were sick, or had been wounded, or perhaps the captain of some vessel banished them there. All of which might make a plot for an interesting story, but so far as actual facts are concerned, there are none to substantiate this line of thinking.

Pirates there probably were, and it is entirely plausible that they should have stopped at Ocracoke for repairs or to replenish supplies. But so far as is known, they didn't leave anybody on the island when they got ready to depart. As I've stated in an earlier chapter, the permanent residents of Ocracoke came there from points up in Virginia.

Spanish galleons, succeeded by other types of sailing craft, enjoyed rich pickings off the coast of America

during the eighteenth century. And, as a matter of fact, even before that, according to some historians. In this connection, permit me to digress just a moment and mention that well-known method of getting rid of prisoners by making them walk the plank. You've heard about that ever since you were able to read stories about pirates and their method of operating, but I believe it has been pretty well established that no pirate ever resorted to any such methods. Why should he, when it was much simpler and much easier to just heave the prisoners overboard?

Walking the plank is just as much of a legend as the story about burning witches in Salem, Mass. No witches ever were burned there.

But getting back to our pirates again; Teache was by no means the only one who marauded the coast of North Carolina, although he undoubtedly is the best known. There were quite a number of others, including two women—Ann Bonney and Mary Read who, judging from accounts, were just about as bloodthirsty characters as ever scuttled a ship.

Ann was the daughter of an Irish lawyer who emigrated to America soon after 1700, prospered and settled down to live in eastern North Carolina. Against her father's wishes, she ran away and secretly married a young sailor who had been a member of Blackbeard's crew. Her father promptly disowned her. Her sailor-husband, finding that he wasn't going to come in for a sizable fortune, left her high and dry. Ann then took up with the notorious pirate, "Calico Jack" Rackam with whom, from all acounts, she seems to have done pretty well for she soon became known as one of the most dangerous members of his crew of cutthroats until they were all seized in 1780 near Jamaica, in the British West Indies.

When they were captured by a British sloop, there

was another woman on board "Calico Jack's" vessel. Her name was Mary Read who had a history even more terrible than that Ann Bonney enjoyed. She had been brought up as a boy with the idea that she would have a better chance in life if she wore breeches, and it is said that she sailed the seas for many years as a sailor before her sex was discovered. Tiring of a buccaneer's life, Mary married a fellow pirate and they kept an inn near Beaufort until she got the wanderlust again, donned her husband's clothing and shipped before the mast on a West India frigate. It was while on this voyage that she was captured by "Calico Jack" Rackam and his rough crew. While on board his vessel she became notorious because of her courage and daring, and on one occasion is said to have fought a duel with another pirate in which she killed her man.

After "Calico Jack" and his crew were captured, both women were tried by British authorities in the West Indies for "audacious crimes and misdemeanors on the high seas" and were sentenced to death. Mary was saved from execution when she contracted a fatal fever while in prison. Ann, who was with child, remained in prison until her baby was born. She was reprieved from time to time and by some trick of justice was finally pardoned.

Besides Rackham, there were Charles Vane, Joe Lawson and Big Jim Braham who infested the waters of North Carolina and are believed to have made Ocracoke their rendezvous on a number of occasions.

The Island's Worst Storm

Storms are no rarity on Ocracoke. The same thing can be said of any other place along the Atlantic seaboard. However, most of the hurricanes that have hit our coast in recent years haven't inflicted any considerable damage on the island. An unusually high tide will sometimes flood low areas but the natives take things of this nature in their stride and don't make any fuss over it.

The most severe storm to have visited Ocracoke in the last sixty years or so occurred during August, 1899. It played havoc along the North Carolina coast, all the way from Southport to Currituck County. Practically all of the outer banks were completely inundated.

"Here's a dispatch about the effects of the storm on Ocracoke, as published by the *Washington Gazette:*

"Washington, N. C., August 21, The whole island of Ocracoke is a complete wreck as a result of the fierce storm which swept the entire coast of North

Carolina, leaving ruin and disaster in its path. The wind reached a velocity of 70 miles an hour, and the sea broke over Ocracoke in waves that were 20 and 30 feet high. Thirty-three homes were destroyed and two churches were wrecked. Practically every house on the island was damaged to some extent.

"Mr. George Buckman, honored citizen of this town, and Henry Blango, colored cook, were drowned.

"A number of boats were sunk or were dashed to pieces against the shore. Word has reached here that there is much suffering on Ocracoke, due to lack of both food and water. A number of families have lost all their possessions. Relief is being sent from here and also from New Bern and other places.

"Much damage also was done on the island of Portsmouth where a number of houses were wrecked."

That was back in 1899. Since then, as I've already said, there have been other storms visiting Ocracoke but in no instance has the damage reached any great extent. As a matter of fact, the mainland of North Carolina has suffered much more severely from hurricanes than has Ocracoke.

If you're planning to spend some time on the island, you don't need to worry about storms: anyway, you don't need to worry any more than you would if you went to any other vacation resort along the Atlantic coast.

Some Historical Information

When the Pilgrims came to this country, where did they land?

Did you say Plymouth Rock?

That's what most of our readers would say if the question were asked them but, of course, it isn't true. The Pilgrims made their first landing at Provincetown near the tip end of Cape Cod. Then, after having caught their breath and resting up a bit, they piled aboard the *Mayflower* again, sailed across the bay and got their feet wet as they slipped off Plymouth Rock.

Now then, where did Sir Walter Raleigh's colonists land when they came to this country?

Most folks would say Roanoke Island, because that's what we have heard for years and years. Actually, however, historical records show that they landed at Woccocon—now Ocracoke—before proceeding on up the coast and finally arriving at Roanoke Island.

Hakluyt's history of the Raleigh expedition testified to this fact in the following statement: "At length, the preparations being completed, a fleet of seven vessels, all small, however, and capable of entering the inlets of Virginia sounds, under command of Sir Richard Grenville . . . set sail from Plymouth, England, April 9, 1585. After various adventures that caused delay, the fleet passed the Cape Feare on June 23d and days later came to anchor at Woccocon, southwest of Cape Hatterask."

Hakluyt doesn't say how long the English people remained at Ocracoke but chances are they stayed at least a few days in order to replenish their supplies and perhaps make some repairs to their vessels.

Ocracoke Inlet, in those days, was the widest and deepest inlet along our coast. All of the early maps show this. During the colonial period the inlet was used extensively by shipping, and the same thing is true of many years thereafter.

Here's some additional historical information about the island:

Ocracoke helped materially in winning the Revolutionary War. It was the only inlet not blockaded by the British fleet, and the French succeeded in bringing in contraband goods across the bar to Pamlico Sound where it was transferred to lighter draft vessels and carried to Bath, Edenton and other places for overland shipment to Washington's forces in the North.

Prior to that—in 1747 or thereabouts—the Spanish invaded Ocracoke and made the inhabitants come across with large numbers of hogs, cattle, chickens and produce of various kinds.

In 1798, along with the appropriation for the first

lighthouse at Cape Hatteras, a similar appropriation was made for the first light at Ocracoke Inlet. It was located on Shell Castle Rock, just off Portsmouth. A storm came along and changed the direction of Wallace Channel, making this lighthouse useless. The present structure was built on Ocracoke Island in 1823.

During the War of 1812, a good deal of privateering was done through Ocracoke Inlet. Otway Burns, who lies buried in the Beaufort cemetery, was a prominent figure in this line of activity.

While the War Between the States was in progress, residents of Ocracoke could hear the thundering of cannon and see the flash of lights while the Battle of Hatteras Inlet was in progress. (I've heard it said that some of the population got mightily scared and started to evacuate and go to Swan Quarter but they changed their minds and decided to stay. Whether this is true or not I can't say.)

During both World War I and World War II, the Coast Guard at Ocracoke played an important part in rescuing survivors from German-torpedoed tankers and other vessels. In the latter war there was an amphibious landing practice unit operated by the Navy, also radar experimentations and Coast Guard activities.

And so, it would seem that the island played a right important part in the various wars in which our country has participated.

Port of Entry

During the early part of the eighteenth century—somewhere about 1715—the Colonial Assembly, realizing the value of Ocracoke Inlet for trade and, at the same time realizing the danger to trade from shoals outside and inside the inlet, passed an act for settling and maintaining pilots at Ocracoke Inlet. These pilots, so far as history discloses, were the first permanent settlers. The earliest history of Ocracoke is chiefly the history of the pilots and their activities.

It is only within comparatively recent years that the duty of piloting vessels in and out from ocean to sound through the treacherous waters of the inlet has been taken over by the U. S. Coast Guard. Prior to that there was the Life Saving Service, and before that were the independent pilots who maintained a long and colorful tradition on the island. There are still a few of the older inhabitants of the island who, in their early years, served as pilots.

In the earliest days, pilots were few in number. In the year 1795 the whole population of the island was but thirty families.

The duty of the pilots was to bring ships safely over

the bar, and so peculiar and shifting were the shoals and channels of Ocracoke Inlet that the task did not lack danger. Pilot fees for every vessel outside the bar into Beacon Island Road were two shillings proclamation money, and for every vessel drawing six feet or less to Bath, thirty-six shillings.

Life among the early pilots was not always happy, nor were they allowed to determine their own rates of collection. Furthermore, it became necessary in 1755 for the General Assembly to enact a penalty fee of ten pounds proclamation money against any pilot at Ocracoke or Beacon Island who, on being signaled, neglected to go over the bar to bring in a vessel. The fee was payable to the master of the vessel detained outside the inlet for want of such a pilot.

That laws of this nature were necessary to make the pilots attend to their business is evidenced by complaints to the colonial governor. An example of this was the report received by Governor Johnston in 1746 to the effect that when Captain Henry Danbus of the frigate *Granville* of London arrived outside the Ocracoke bar from Cork, bringing news of the defeat of the Scots at Colloden, he lay exposed outside the inlet and in danger of privateers, the pilots failing to come to his assistance.

It is of interest that in those days, as in modern times, the forces of nature were constantly changing the contour of the Carolina reefs. In 1764 it was necessary for the colony to set aside more land for the homes of the pilots inasmuch as the land originally used for this purpose had been washed away.

In appropriating this land for the use of the pilots, the colonial assembly included in the Act of 1764 the requirement that no pilot should keep running at large any cattle or livestock "to the prejudice of the present proprietors." That this law was not obeyed is clear from subsequent history, since a notable annual event on the island for many years has been the Fourth-of-July roundup of wild ponies and cattle. In fact, the old colonial law has long been forgotten and in recent years has been replaced by a new ruling of the federal government outlawing unfenced livestock on the banks in an attempt to grass the outer banks and develop the seashore park. Up to the present time, however, the few remaining ponies are still at large.

The Gallivantin'
Outer Banks

This old world of ours, after having gone through many geological changes, is pretty well established.

If you're a resident of Charlotte, if you were to pull up stakes and move out to California, and if you should return in thirty years or more, you'd be pretty sure that Charlotte would be exactly where it was when you left it. Of course the city might have grown a lot but this growth would be in the nature of expansion in all directions.

The same thing is true of practically every other place—except the outer banks, of which Ocracoke is a part.

Throughout the years there have been many changes along this strip of narrow islands along the coast of North Carolina. The beach has been built up at some points, it has been washed away at others. Sand dunes move slowly up the coast, the sand being blown up one side and deposited on the other. It was because of this that the memorial to the Wright brothers on Kill

Devil Hill couldn't be built until it had been "anchored" by planting grass on its slopes. Prior to that it kept inching up toward the north.

Inlets appear after a severe storm while others vanish. The same is true of channels. Many years ago someone may have left a worn-out automobile on the sand-flats: today it may be a sizable sand dune.

These changes have been recognized as one of the nation's major geographic curiosities. They are fascinating to the layman and expert alike.

The present shoreline has been built up by wave action on what originally were shoals situated farther to the east. The outer banks are now being pushed toward the mainland by wave action, which washes the sand to the beach, and by wind action, which carries the sand inland. The winds are constantly moving the sand, building dunes and ridges in some places and tearing them down in others. This movement will continue as long as the sea remains at its present level.

Some 20,000 years ago, the shoreline was far back on the mainland. Let's say that it was where Washington, New Bern, Columbia and Elizabeth City are now located. The water level was 25 feet above its present level. Then came the last glaciation and the water level dropped 50 feet, or 25 feet lower than at present. This meant that such shallow areas as Diamond Shoals were completely out of water. As a matter of fact, I've heard Frank Kugler of Washington say that even in recent years he has jumped out of a boat at Diamond Shoals and has walked on dry sand. The final step was when the continental ice sheet melted and the sea level rose to its present height. This meant that many low areas, formerly out of water, became submerged again.

It's an interesting study. And don't think for a moment that the changes are at an end. Not by a long shot; they will continue as long as the waves wash on the beach and as long as the wind blows the sand around.

The New Road

During the early part of 1955, Governor Luther Hodges made a trip to Ocracoke and invited me—along with several others—to go along.

We flew in a National Guard airplane to Cherry Point and then transferred to helicopters. Landing on the island was made close to the Coast Guard Station.

A motorcade proceeded part-way up the island and the Governor was shown where the people of Ocracoke wanted a new, hard-surfaced road built.

Various people talked to him about the project. They pointed out that Ocracoke was being neglected, that many more people would come to the island if better means of transportation was afforded them, that they were having to live in one of the most isolated communities in the entire state, that if other sections of North Carolina were being provided with good roads there was no reason why Ocracoke shouldn't have a decent highway.

The Governor listened attentively.

Then we went to the Wahab Village Hotel where a luncheon was served to fifty or sixty people. This was followed by a meeting in the recreation hall at the schoolhouse. Two hundred or more folks were present. Those who couldn't get inside, hung around the windows and doors in order to hear what the Governor had to say.

Governor Hodges made his speech. Toward the end of it he promised that he would recommend to the State Highway Commission the construction of a practicable hard-surfaced road.

No speaker on the island has ever been accorded the applause that the Governor received upon making this statement.

The contract for construction of the highway was let the early part of the year and practically all of the road was completed during 1957. This means that if you wish to drive to the island you now can do so without any special difficulty. Bridge across Oregon Inlet, paved road down Hatteras Island, ferry across Hatteras Inlet and paved road down Ocracoke Island to the village of Ocracoke.

National Seashore Rec-
reational Area

A big change has come over Ocracoke as a result of
the island having been included in the Cape Hatteras
National Seashore Park.

The National Park Service has acquired possession
of practically all of the island with the exception of
the area included in the Village of Ocracoke. And this,
in itself, is only a small portion of the park which
extends from Whalebone Junction at the southern
boundary of Nags Head to the southern tip of Ocracoke
Island. This means that the Park Service has taken
over control of 28,500 acres of land. It is divided into
three sections on three islands—Bodie, Hatteras and
Ocracoke, each separated from its neighbor by an
inlet. Ocracoke was the last area acquired.

The act of Congress, dated August 17, 1937,
authorizing the establishment of the National Seashore
Recreational Area, states that "except for certain por-
tions of the area, deemed to be especially adaptable
for recreational uses, particularly swimming, boating,
sailing, fishing and other recreational activities of

216

similar nature, which shall be developed for such uses as needed, the said area shall be permanently reserved as a primitive wilderness and no development of the project or plan for the convenience of visitors shall be undertaken which would be incompatible with the preservation of the unique flora and fauna or the physiographic conditions now prevailing in the area."

That's one of the longest sentences we've come across in a long time.

The act was later amended in several ways. Sport fishing is allowed without any restrictions whatsoever. Commercial fishing is permitted to legal residents of the island within boundaries determined by the Park Service so far as hauling of nets is concerned. It is generally understood that fishing in boats may continue as usual (commercial fishing, that is) but there may be some curtailment about dragging nets in areas reserved for bathing. Of course the chances are that nothing will ever come up about this because there isn't much net dragging except during the winter months when there is no bathing.

Hunting is definitely allowed in blinds except on Pea Island, further up the coast. It also will be permitted on the land on Ocracoke Island and probably at one or two other places.

Here's what is behind all this:

The Park Service feels that more and more beach property is being developed by private parties to the exclusion of the public at large. You see many evidences of this up in the New England States as well as in other parts of the country.

217

The Park Service decided it was time to put a stop to this: that action should be taken whereby large tracts of coastal land and beaches would be preserved for the use of John Q. Public and his family.

So the acquisition of land got under way and this included Ocracoke.

The villages along the outer banks included in the park area are not affected. They'll be allowed to continue operations the same as before, with sizable expansion room around each to permit independent growth as tourist centers.

You've read elsewhere in this book about the wild ponies and cattle that roam the island at large. Well, they may soon be passing out of the picture. As this is being written, the Park Service has decided that the cattle must go. Whether the horses also will have to be penned up in the village or removed from the island entirely remains to be seen. However the latest information I have been able to obtain is that the ponies will be allowed to remain.

The Park Service program will be principally one of preservation: to keep the seashore area as it is. Some folks have the idea that tourist homes, hot-dog stands, filling stations, etc., will be built up from one end of the park to the other, but such is not the case. The Park Service doesn't contemplate anything like that. It will, however, select points of particular recreational, scenic or historical interest and make them more easily accessible through construction of parking areas and approach roads. Two locations have been designated where rough camping is now permitted.

218

One of these is at Oregon Inlet and the other near the point at Cape Hatteras. A third has been laid out on Ocracoke. Hunting areas also will be designated. Aside from this, most of Ocracoke Island will remain as it now is; the big change, if any, will come in or adjacent to the village. The same is true of the communities farther up the banks.

But probably the outstanding work that the Cape Hatteras National Seashore Park is doing consists of planting grass and building up the sand dunes, thereby preventing as much erosion as possible.

And That's Ocracoke

As best I could, I have tried to bring you what I believe is a fairly comprehensive and accurate picture of the island and its people.

If you are among those who have been there, I hope you have enjoyed the description of things that undoubtedly are familiar to you. If you never have been there, I hope that what I have written may create a desire to see the island for yourself.

If you want to rest
In peace and quiet,
Here's the place
For you to try it.
Forget your cares,
Your worries, too,
And just relax,
The whole day through.
It makes no difference
If you're rich or broke,
You'll enjoy your rest
At Ocracoke.